Calm your anxiety and take back control

||| | ||||||||| ||| |||||| |||| |||
I0115913

...

Calm Anxiety

Taking Back Control

TERRY DIXON

Help-For

Published by Help-For
www.help-for.com

A catalogue record for this book is available at the British Library
ISBN 978 0 9558136 8 9

Important: The information in this book is not intended to be used
for self-diagnosis nor to be taken as a substitute for good individual
personal professional medical attention. The only intent of the author
is to offer information to help you in your quest for well-being and no
responsibility can be taken by the author or publisher for the way this
information is used.

It is strongly recommended that anyone who is thinking, feeling or
behaving in a way that they don't understand, any way that is causing
pain or unhappiness, should consult a medical professional and that a
medical doctor should always be consulted for any persistent physical
or bodily function problem, in the first instance, to rule out possible
physical causes before psychological reasons are explored. And that,
under no circumstances, should anybody stop taking prescribed
medication without fully qualified medical supervision.

To everyone struggling with anxiety.

...

CONTENTS

...

INTRODUCTION

"I HAVE ANXIETY, I have a mental illness." We're not quite at this stage yet but we are getting there.

The speeding heart and rapid breathing, the sweating, trembling, feeling 'on-edge' and that sense of impending danger are all extremely powerful. They descend upon us without warning and we cannot seem to stop them. These thoughts, feelings and behaviours, over which we have virtually no control, affect us deeply – and they are supposed to, for if we had to consciously prepare for fighting or fleeing it would be too late.

Anxiety is a vital part of being human. Indeed, every living organism on the planet has its own form of anxiety, its very own built-in self-protection instinct. Essentially to help us survive, to keep us alive, it sits quietly in the background waiting to spring into action when needed in times of danger. We all have anxiety; it's with us to some extent for most of the time and we can see examples of it in action daily:-

- Without anxiety over being knocked down we wouldn't be careful when we crossed the road.
- Without anxiety over losing food and shelter we wouldn't continue to go to a job we hate each day.

Such powerful feelings and so little control – it's no wonder that anxiety can be seen as an awful problem, a terrible weakness, something that has to be eradicated from our lives at all cost. But it can't be. It's part of us.

It was Mark Twain who said, "Courage is resistance to fear, mastery of fear – not absence of fear." We cannot remove fear from our life. Similarly, self-confidence and feelings of security come from the mastery of anxiety, resistance to anxiety – not the absence of it.

"He has not learned the lesson of life who does not every day surmount a fear."

...Gaius Julius Caesar (100–44 B.C.)

When we understand and accept our anxiety we begin to take control. Rather counter-intuitively: acceptance controls anxiety, fighting it makes it worse. Mastery of anxiety enables us to live life to the full and most of us start out this way... until life takes hold.

Once anxiety starts to control us, things change. It can lead to a whole host of serious debilitating problems –

problems classified as 'anxiety disorders' and 'mental illness' today.

The start of these problems is often a period of prolonged increased anxiety, seemingly without cause. Numerous research studies have shown that the one thing most people suffering from long-term anxiety disorders remember about the start of their problem is: "being too nervous for a long time".

This book is about just that: 'being too nervous (or too anxious) for a long time without good reason'. It is to help you understand why this happens and how to deal with it – how to take control of such anxiety rather than letting it control you – and in doing so nip any potential future problems in the bud.

In Part I we'll look at the current beliefs and theories about anxiety-related problems and how they influence everything we think about anxiety.

In Part II we'll explore anxiety through the lens of human evolution and survival. What is it? Why do we have it? How does it work? Here, you'll discover the real reason for that increased anxiety that plagues so many of us today.

Part III will teach you how to take control of anxiety and master it. This can make the difference between a life ruled by fear or one lived with confidence, so let's get started and take a look at how we think about anxiety today...

...

PART I

ANXIETY TODAY

...

1

The Medical Model

TODAY, ACROSS THE world, millions and millions of people struggle valiantly with problems involving anxiety. Ranging from increased nervousness through to crippling anxiety disorders and severe depression, these problems are fast becoming the number one health concern in many countries.

It is estimated that in America alone over 40 million people suffer from some form of anxiety disorder. The most common one is social anxiety disorder (also called social phobia), closely followed by post traumatic stress disorder (PTSD) and generalized anxiety disorder (GAD). Around one in thirty to fifty people suffer from obsessive compulsive disorder (OCD) and one in ten are reported to have a specific phobia. This doesn't include vast numbers of people who have depression or those living anxious lives ruled by shyness or stress.

Many people feel they are working well below their potential and are unhappy and frustrated, more people are unhealthy and overweight than ever before, greater numbers of teenagers are depressed and problems involving anxiety and stress account for the majority of visits to doctor's surgeries. In a world of better food, hygiene, education and healthcare – emotionally, society is crumbling.

The Oxford English Dictionary defines anxiety as: *'a feeling of worry, nervousness, or unease about something with an uncertain outcome'* but it is more than just a feeling. It also involves our thoughts and the way we act. The list below reflects this.

Anxiety Symptoms

These are associated with avoiding and/or dealing with danger and involve our body, mind and behaviour.

Our body:-

- Breathing becomes more rapid.
- Heartbeat speeds up.
- We feel dizzy and light-headed.
- We get 'butterflies' in our stomach.
- We feel sick and/or need the toilet.

- Our mouth becomes dry and it feels difficult to swallow.
- We sweat more.
- We feel 'jittery' / 'jumpy' / 'on-edge'.

Our thoughts:-

- We feel frightened.
- We may tell ourselves that we are physically ill, having a heart attack or a stroke or going mad.
- We think people are looking at us.
- We worry that we may lose control or make a fool of ourselves in front of others.
- We feel that we must escape and get to a safe place.

Our behaviour:-

- We make excuses to avoid going out or doing things.
- We hurry out of places or situations where we feel anxious.
- We walk to avoid buses or cross the street to avoid people.
- We may have a drink or take a tablet before doing something we find stressful.

Anxiety is a part of being human; we all have it. And to get anxious in certain situations is normal, everyone does. Most people even experience increased anxiety frequently. Things like tests, interviews, public speaking, first dates and competitive sports can make anyone pretty anxious.

But for some of us things change, our anxiety grows stronger. It comes on more and more and seems to happen for no apparent reason.

Many people live like this, in a state of heightened anxiety, feeling apprehensive and 'on-edge' frequently, often getting 'too-scared' in various life situations. Physical symptoms due to anxiety may appear.

For others, over time, this increased anxiety can lead to whole host of more serious problems if not resolved – awful problems such as excessive and uncontrollable worrying, anxiety attacks or panic attacks that come 'out of the blue', irrational fears and phobias (particularly social phobia), obsessive thoughts and compulsive behaviours even severe depression... problems we know today as anxiety disorders.

The medical definition of a disorder is: *'an illness that disrupts normal physical or mental functions'*. Anxiety disorders are characterised by significant feelings of anxiety and fear and there are five main types classified today:-

1. Generalized Anxiety Disorder

Generalized Anxiety Disorder (GAD) involves long-lasting exaggerated and unrealistic worry, mainly over things pertaining to the health and personal safety of our self and family members. It is often accompanied by general feelings of apprehension and being 'on-edge' for much of the time.

Having generalized anxiety disorder is like being in a constant state of 'what if...?' We experience increased, persistent anxiety (seemingly for no apparent reason) and so live in a constant state of apprehension and fear over something bad happening.

Physically, we frequently feel 'on-edge' and 'jittery' and live in a state of increased tension. Our senses, heart rate and blood pressure are higher than normal. Over time this state of increased physiological arousal often leads to fatigue, lethargy and feeling generally 'run down', which can result in constant colds, flus and illness. After a while, being in a state of constant tension can cause numerous aches and pains in our body.

Mentally, the excessive feelings of anxiety result in constant worrying ("we are so anxious... why? What's going to happen? What can I do about it?") and we start to obsess uncontrollably about bad things that may happen. This worry can be over many things: bad things that may happen in the future or may happen because of something we have done in the past. A common worry revolves around the greatest fear that almost everyone has deep down, that is the fear that something awful may happen to our loved ones.

2. Obsessive Compulsive Disorder

Obsessive compulsive disorder (OCD) is characterised by persistent, upsetting thoughts that we cannot control (obsessions) and actions that we feel compelled to do, seemingly against our own will (compulsions). In most cases we are driven to do the compulsive behaviours in order to alleviate the anxiety caused by the obsessive thoughts. For example, if we just can't get it out of our mind that something is dirty (even if it isn't really) we will clean it incessantly no matter how clean it actually is.

In the early 16th century, *'obsession'* referred to a siege or 'laying siege to' and that's just what our intrusive thoughts do to us. They besiege us.

Constantly intruding into our mind against our will, we cannot prevent them, change them or make them go away and it can be extremely distressing. Common obsessions include: blasphemous thoughts, harming a loved one, obscene thoughts and exaggerated fears over such things as contamination and dirt, aggression and violence or religion and sex.

The thoughts themselves can make us feel bad but we also feel really bad because we cannot control them.

Often the obsessive thoughts lead to compulsive behaviours and again, as with the obsessions, we feel a total lack of control while performing the compulsive act. We know that what we are doing is wrong and that we're blowing the fear out of all proportion but we cannot stop. We cannot stop even though our actions may be hurting us and feel compelled to continue with the behaviour at all cost, because if we stop doing it the thing that we dread happening might just happen.

3. Post Traumatic Stress Disorder

Post traumatic stress disorder (PTSD) is characterised by the re-living of traumatic events through such things as flashbacks or nightmares. It involves not only extreme anxiety but also emotional numbing as we try and deal with the stress induced by the traumatic event(s).

Whether experienced personally or as a witness, traumatic events can have a very powerful effect on us. They hit home in a very real, imminent and shocking way just how vulnerable we really are. Commonly associated with war veterans (with good reason) we don't have to experience the horrors of war to develop PTSD. Anything that induces hurt, fear and shock can do the same. Constant abuse (both physical and mental) can be a very common cause.

With such a threat to our existence, flashbacks and nightmares represent our mind trying to deal with the situation, to re-live it and come to some peace over it. Unlike many anxiety disorders where the dangers are usually generated in our mind, with PTSD the danger is real (we have actually experienced it) and it is out there.

A very real threat to our survival remains unresolved. This is why it is so intolerable.

4. Social Anxiety Disorder (Social Phobia)

With social anxiety disorder we fear situations where we have to do things in front of others and there is the possibility that they may judge, ridicule or reject us. It's not about being a bit shy or a bit embarrassed about it or that we feel apprehensive about doing things in front of others, it's that we are panic-stricken. Indeed, we can often feel as scared about doing some task in front of other people as if we were going to face a firing squad.

Social anxiety disorder is also known as social phobia and like all phobias it involves anticipatory anxiety, fear and panic when facing the object or situation that scares us.

Imagine someone who has a phobia of spiders and panics whenever they have to face one. Replace the spider with people and having to face them (or do things in front of them) – this is what it feels like to have social anxiety disorder.

Rooted in the deep and real instinctual fears of our primitive ancestors, where a fear of strangers was necessary for survival (for they may attack us, steal from us or kill us) and rejection from the tribe could lead to isolation and death, the main focus of modern day social anxiety disorder is rejection.

5. Panic Disorder

The focus here is on attacks of panic that appear to come on without cause. Involving a racing heartbeat (palpitations), chest pain, sweating, trembling and shaking, many people fear that they are having a heart attack or stroke, dying or going mad.

Our heart beats so fast that our chest shudders; we can hear it, we can feel it. We are breathing rapidly and our shoulders are raised and tense. Our legs feel like jelly and our arms and hands tremble, we can't keep them still. What's wrong with us? Why is this happening? We feel sick and want to go to the toilet, our mouth is dry, it's hard to swallow and we are sweating. Feelings of dread consume us and we have an overwhelming urge to run, to flee, to get away.

All of this and out of the blue... no wonder we feel that there is something radically wrong with us.

*

The preceding five types of problem reflect the current classification of anxiety disorders as it stands today. However, when we fully understand anxiety we come to realise that it doesn't stop there. Indeed, virtually everything we know as a mental 'disorder' can be traced back to find anxiety at its root.

Body dysmorphic disorder and personality disorders, bipolar disorder and eating disorders, over-eating (comfort eating) and yo-yo dieting, increased sensitivity to stress at home, at school or in the workplace... an undercurrent of unresolved anxiety flows through all of these problems and more.

And there is another problem in particular, one that has reached almost epidemic proportions and also has anxiety at its core. That problem is depression and it really should be included in the list.

6. Depression (Severe)

It's important to realise that, like anxiety, depression in itself is not an illness. Depression is an integral part of being human; everybody gets depressed to some degree at certain times in his or her life.

Life throws many things at us that give us a good right to become depressed. Such things as the death of a loved one, prolonged illness or incapacity, and long-term relationship problems bring home to us our lack of control. This lack of control makes us feel helpless and hopeless and that there's nothing we can do to change things. This is normal depression.

However, there is a situation where depression goes much deeper and becomes associated with something more than just those awful life events that are uncontrollable and happen to everyone. Yes the same bad things happen, but they become related to our very self, our 'weakness' and the belief that there is nothing we can do about it. With severe depression, nothing sounds good and nothing feels good, thinking processes slow down and are replaced by a lack of concentration, indecisiveness and rumination. Dullness descends over us such that even colours can appear faded.

Depress means *'to press down'* and deep depression results from a 'pushing down' of emotions and feelings, particularly anger. Our mind and body symbolise this dullness and 'pressing down', and make it real to us through physical sensations such as 'a weight on our shoulders' or 'a thick fog surrounding us'. Depression involves tiredness and body aches, lethargy and procrastination, and our depressed immune system often results in constant colds, flus and viruses. In chronic depression the only real things we do feel include anxiety and fear, worthlessness, helplessness, hopelessness and guilt.

* * *

The medical model (from which this definition of a disorder: *'an illness that disrupts normal physical or mental functions'* derives) considers all the problems described above to be just that... an illness. It views anxiety disorders and depression as something going physically wrong (in the brain) and the answer lies in 'fixing' the thing that has gone wrong – usually with medication.

In itself, the term 'illness' suggests something that just happens to us, some awful thing that we were just unlucky enough to fall foul of. Nothing could be further from the truth.

As you know, we don't simply wake up one day with these problems. They start off slowly and get stronger and stronger over time. Few of us, if any, had anxiety issues as a child. It's usually just the opposite. Yet something happens that turns the confidence we had as children into anxiety. Something happens that takes away our confidence and fills us with insecurity, so much insecurity that anxiety (our self-protection system) kicks in.

There is no real mystery to anxiety disorders. Their development follows a logical psychological progression and we can map out what happens every step of the way. Yet the prevailing worldview continues to promote them as 'something going wrong' (that needs fixing) and proposes a number of ideas and theories about what it is that has actually gone wrong.

Although unproven, these ideas and theories have become widely accepted as fact and often form the basis of treatment for many anxiety disorders today. Let's examine them more closely:-

Perhaps it's because our brain is different or works differently to other people's?

PET (Positron Emission Tomography) brain scans of people with OCD show increased energy use in the orbital cortex of the brain compared to those who don't have OCD. This has led to the assumption that people have obsessive compulsive disorder because their brains are different (larger, more active) in certain areas than people who don't have the disorder – an assumption that has progressed to many disorders and possibly even anxiety problems in general.

Well, brain scans of violinists show the area of the brain devoted to his or her left fingers (the right primary motor cortex) to be 2 or 3 times larger than that of non-violinists. Constant use of these fingers in playing the violin have formed and embedded the associated pattern of connections in the musician's brain making it larger and more active in these areas.

There can be little doubt that constant obsessive thinking and frequent episodes of acting compulsively will embed the associated neural patterns in our brain, altering it in respect to both size (the strength and number of connections) and activity. OCD causes the change in our brain – it's not the other way round.

Maybe we have a chemical imbalance in our brain?

Synapses are connections between the neurons in our brain; there are around 10,000 for each neuron. They are tiny spaces that are occupied by chemical messengers called neurotransmitters that carry information between neurons.

The chemicals serotonin and dopamine are two main neurotransmitters regularly mentioned with regard to many anxiety and depression problems. And a chemical imbalance, usually referring to deficiencies of these neurotransmitters, is often proffered as a reason for these problems. This is despite there being a lack of any real evidence to support it.

Anxiety and depression deplete our body of many resources, including such things as energy, vitamins, minerals, electrolytes and no doubt neurotransmitters. Surely, any chemical imbalance is the result of these problems not the cause. Balancing chemicals in the brain through the action of prescription drugs may alleviate some of the symptoms temporarily but doesn't address the underlying reason for the problem.

[Looking at the chemical imbalance situation from this perspective may offer an explanation for one of the most terrible aspects of taking medication for depression... suicide, a known side-effect for some anti depressants. Mercifully rare, considering any chemical imbalance as being a result of depression (not the cause of it) offers an answer to this.

If we accept that serotonin is associated in some way to feeling good, then, when life throws awful things at us that makes us depressed our body (brain) will use more of it to try and make us feel better. This may result in over-usage and a diminished amount of serotonin in our system. Prescription antidepressants such as SSRIs, in an attempt to keep the serotonin levels higher, prevent us from using it (reabsorbing it) possibly when we really need to, maybe desperately. Perhaps a better way would be to increase serotonin levels by making more (naturally) rather than keeping levels high by preventing its usage?]

Anxiety and depression are inextricably interlinked and antidepressants are often prescribed for anxiety. However, whatever the reason, balancing chemicals only deals with symptoms and never touches the actual cause.

Before we go on, I'd like to reiterate a very important point made at the beginning of this book. With respect to the previous section and the upcoming section on beta-blockers... *Under no circumstance should anyone stop taking prescription medication without full medical supervision.*

Or is it all in our genes?

Human beings are very complex. If all of the DNA (deoxyribonucleic acid) in your body were laid end to end it would reach to the sun and back over 600 times.

Genes are pieces of DNA passed from parent to offspring that contain hereditary information. A parent and child share 50% of their genes as do siblings. Identical twins share 100% of their genes.

Once the human genome was mapped (the entire DNA sequence that makes up humans) it was hoped to be able to identify and cure the genetic cause of almost any problem. But that didn't happen. Whilst ground has been made identifying DNA mutations or variations that may be associated with a higher risk for certain diseases, the actual situation is a great deal more complex. The position of the genes in relation to other genes and the interactions between them may exert as great an influence as the genes themselves. It's the structure as a whole, the system, not just its constituent parts that is important. Anxiety and depression problems are the same, it is the whole system that counts – our mind and body and the environment they are in.

If a person has survived in life despite an existence racked by worry, compulsions or depression, it's not unreasonable to assume that these survival 'tactics' will be passed to his or her offspring in order to increase their chances of survival. A lifelong depressive, no doubt, passes genetic information appropriate to having depression to any offspring.

However, DNA is our past and not our future. Information that is passed between a parent and child does not result in actual behaviours, but predispositions, not fixed behaviours but ways of behaving we are susceptible to develop given the right stimulation. A parent cannot pass on fixed behaviours for the environment the child is born into is unknown and the knowledge we inherit has to flexible to enable us to adapt and survive. Reacting with extreme anxiety to unconditional love would not be adaptive.

We all come predisposed to learn language, but the main language we eventually learn to speak depends on where in the world we are born. Racehorses are bred to be good runners but they still have to be groomed and trained. Any genetic information that we receive from our parents can only be put into practice if the appropriate environment exists.

Complex interactions between predisposition and environment probably influence the development of many anxiety-related problems (and the strength of the problem) but it's the environment, our experiences, that holds the upper hand. Genetic influence sits quietly in the background waiting to develop and flourish given the right circumstances or wither and die if not called upon.

There is also evidence to suggest that genes can be altered through learning.

The popular belief among scientists has been that although the environment influenced natural selection, mutation was random. This is to say that environmental changes may favour certain characteristics of a species such that only those members that possess such characteristics survive to pass on their genes, but genetic changes were purely random. It happened by chance and may or may not confer benefits for survival.

However, experiments by Barbara McClintock in the 1950's showed vast changes in the DNA of plants occurring when they were stressed. A stressful environment actually resulted in whole sequences of DNA moving from one place to another, even inserting themselves into active genes. Not random behaviour, there was a method to their shifting and it was triggered by outside influences (changes in the environment such as extreme heat or drought) that threatened the survival of the plant. Initially ignored by her peers, McClintock received a Nobel Prize for her work some thirty years later.

Genes were changing due to experience in plants – imagine what may be happening within the complexity of humans.

Intuitively, we would expect this to be the case. Life is about growing, learning and evolving; genes shape our reaction to experiences and our reaction to experiences and learning must shape our genes. We need not be slaves to our genes!

* * *

To accept anxiety problems as 'disorders' relies solely on the medical definition, which is based on the premise that they are illnesses. And the word itself: 'dis-order' leads to the acceptance that something is out of order and that we are behaving illogically and irrationally.

But this just isn't the case. Anxiety increases for a reason: to protect us. It serves to warn us that something is not right in our life and we need to change it or get away from it. Our mind and body are perfectly ordered in what they are trying to do and we develop these problems for the most rational reason there will ever be... for our survival.

Anxiety-related problems develop from our survival instincts trying to protect us from being hurt (or worse) and, given individual life experiences, the minds of most people who struggle with these problems are working perfectly normally and rationally – but they are not working appropriately.

Anxiety is a very powerful instinct since our survival depends on it. And it does indeed make us feel awful, weak and scared. Being frightened feels bad, it has to, in order to keep us away from danger.

When we experience anxiety inappropriately (or so it seems) it's perfectly understandable that we may start to think, "What is wrong with me?" and "Why is this happening?" Anyone would think the same.

However, if the answer to these questions involves labels such as 'disorder' and 'mental illness' and theories about causation over which we have little or no control, it's easy to become drawn into a self-defeating belief system about anxiety problems – one that shapes not only the problem but also our entire life.

...

2

"What We Think, We Become"
(Buddha)

A MAN FOUND an eagle's egg and put it in a nest of a barnyard hen. The eaglet hatched with the brood of chicks and grew up with them.

All his life the eagle did what the barnyard chicks did, thinking he was a barnyard chicken. He scratched the earth for worms and insects. He clucked and cackled and would thrash his wings and fly a few feet into the air. Years passed and the eagle grew very old.

One day he saw a magnificent bird above him in the cloudless sky. It glided in graceful majesty among the powerful wind currents, with scarcely a beat of its strong golden wings. The eagle looked up in awe. "Who's that?" he asked. "That's the eagle, the king of the birds," said his neighbour. "He belongs to the sky. We belong to the earth – we're chickens." So the eagle lived and died a chicken, for that's what he thought he was.

This great little story from 'Awareness' by Anthony de Mello makes a very powerful point: often what we believe to be true isn't, even though everything around us appears to support it.

Classifying Anxiety Problems

Categorisation reflects the way the brain and mind work and forms the basis of everything we understand. New information is analysed, compared and stored by reference to what we already know so that we can use it to understand, predict and control our environment. The classification of anxiety disorders is no different; it serves to describe and order various symptoms into well-defined categories to help manage them. This has promoted much research and expanded our knowledge of these problems, however most of the research is limited to what can be physically measured and we can truly measure very little in our universe.

The names given: OCD, GAD, PTSD etc. are only descriptions of ways of thinking, feeling and behaving but naming them gives them a life of their own, a whole new power. Suddenly they are an entity, they exist, and what we think of them is influenced by what we are told. Thoughts and behaviours fundamental to human existence and survival (experienced by all in times of insecurity) that have become exaggerated due to negative life experiences are now deemed a 'disorder' and we start to believe everything that the experts and authorities tell us about them.

Feelings, labels and well-meaning mis-information now interplay to shape our beliefs about anxiety-related problems in such a way that make them seem almost insurmountable.

How many 'normal' people (that is those who don't suffer from increased anxiety, obsessions, compulsions, phobias etc.):-

- Say 'Touch Wood' so as not to tempt fate?
- Repeatedly check doors, windows and switches?
- Take a drink before social functions?
- Avoid public speaking at all cost?

Almost everyone displays behaviours associated with anxiety disorders at some time in his or her life – usually in times of stress for they represent self-protection.

Let's say I normally check the locks on my front door and back door twice before going to bed, once to lock them and once again just to be sure.

Then I hear vague reports of burglaries in the area and I start re-checking the door locks twice. Three times in total I now check each door.

Suddenly I discover for a fact that my next-door neighbour has been burgled and everything changes. I check both doors three times before going upstairs then come down and check them another twice before getting into bed. That's ten times in total.

Now I ask you… have I suddenly developed a mental illness?

Of course not, my self-protective behaviour has become exaggerated due to a clear and present danger and everything I do is perfectly understandable and reasonable.

Before we continue, let's delve more deeply into this type of behaviour, one that often increases in times of stress and is associated with many anxiety problems, that is: rituals.

Rituals: Trying to Control the Uncontrollable

We all have an innate connection to something more, some greater power that we feel may be good to us or do us harm. Nobody wants to tempt fate. Rituals are a part of everyday life, seen in such things as: saying 'touch wood' not to tempt fate; throwing salt over the shoulder; saying 'bless you' after sneezing (to protect from attack by the devil in a vulnerable moment) and all those pre-performance 'ceremonies' of entertainers and sports stars in order to enlist the help of some higher force and be successful. There are worship rituals, greeting rituals, bedroom rituals and eating rituals – all performed so that things go well.

When fears involve potential threats from higher powers and unseen forces, the only thing we can do to allay anxiety involves ordering and rituals. Rituals are basically attempts to control the uncontrollable, to gain a say in the unpredictable.

Ancient tribes, with no understanding of the natural forces that dictated their lives (for example: the sun which provided light, heat and even life itself) often performed rituals to these forces in order to allay the anxiety of having no control whatsoever over the awesome powers that controlled their existence.

The sun, moon and the elements were often seen as gods in many civilisations and, today, all religions perform rituals to God in order to feel a sense of control and gain favour with the ultimate power that can determine our future for eternity.

When we start to lose control, rituals with their inherent structure and order are often the first things to which we turn.

Classification of anxiety 'disorders' also obscures the bigger picture. In focusing on individual categories (disorders), separate reasons and answers are often proffered for each problem yet they are all related. Feelings of insecurity, uncontrollable thoughts and physiological symptoms of anxiety and panic lie at the heart of them all.

Within the disorders themselves there are many similar thoughts, feelings and behaviours.

GAD and OCD both involve self-perpetuating thoughts relating to insecurity and attempts to gain control. Phobias and OCD entail panic when confronted by the feared object or thought.

Feelings of inability to cope with negative events occur with anxiety and depression, but those with depression feel responsible and helpless about the events while those with anxiety generally do not.

Panic disorder, phobias and PTSD all involve some form of avoidance, ranging from that due to the overwhelming urge to escape in phobias (physical avoidance) to the cognitive avoidance strategies used in panic disorders (mental avoidance) and the emotional numbing seen in PTSD to avoid painful feelings (emotional avoidance).

All disorders involve intense feelings of losing control.

Rather than individual disorders it may be better to consider these problems as the outward expression of one main underlying problem. That is increased anxiety, and it is brought about by feelings of insecurity.

* * *

As we are drawn into the world of specific disorders and mental illness we fall naturally into treatment methods that are associated with these beliefs.

The medical model, where physical abnormalities are used to explain our mental processes, goes hand-in-hand with classification and treatment. It provides a neat set of symptoms, well defined and named, often with a neat, specially developed drug to cure them.

Anxiety Problems and Medication

Most of us trust everything the doctor tells us. If he or she tells us (in good faith) that we have an illness we generally accept it. And it may appear to serve us well to accept it – a name for our problem and, in one sense, a relief. It's not our fault but a faulty gene or a chemical imbalance, an illness we were just unfortunate to contract, nothing at all to do with problems in our life.

But this answer doesn't work for long since it ignores the incredible power of the human mind and in doing so doesn't even come close to providing a solution.

In viewing it as merely brain and body and individual parts that have gone wrong and need fixing, once again the bigger picture is overlooked. Medication works on a physical (physiological) level, anxiety problems are psychological and the answer is psychological.

Please remember that under no circumstances should anyone stop taking prescribed medication without medical supervision for it can be dangerous.

Medication has its uses. When we are overwhelmed by anxiety, fears or despair, the appropriate short-term medication can alleviate those symptoms and give us the relief we need to start tackling the problem correctly.

Short-term medication can be a lifesaver; long-term usage of medication generally serves to make things worse for it fuels the very core of the problem. It strengthens our inner feelings of insecurity and weakness. We have to take a tablet to be okay therefore we must be weak. Having to take medication at all (to be 'normal') confirms our inner self-doubt.

Also, if medication has calmed us, once we stop taking it, any anxiety that we experience will feel greater for we are used to being calm. Withdrawal from medication can result in many anxiety symptoms feeling worse, again strengthening the underlying problem. Yet we are turning into a society that is dependent on medication where emotional and life issues have now become illnesses that merit treatment, usually in the form of a pill.

With problems that are defined by anxiety, fear and despair, it would nice if they could be just taken away, removed from us without further struggle – but they cannot. Medication may have some short-term benefits but it can never be a cure for anything related to anxiety.

Bearing this in mind, it may be prudent to take a look at one anxiety medication in particular. This is fast becoming the new panacea for anxiety, dished out with amazing ease and regularity to anyone who mentions the word 'anxiety' when sitting in front of a doctor.

Taking Beta Blockers for Anxiety

Beta blockers reduce the effects of adrenaline in the body and today many people are prescribed these drugs to help deal with anxiety.

In times of stress and emergency the adrenal gland produces adrenaline (a stress hormone) that acts on various organs in the body to enable us to deal with the situation. For example, the heart beats faster due to adrenaline.

In order for adrenaline to be able to do this, these organs have receptors (known as beta receptors) to accept the adrenaline and use it to behave differently in times of stress. Beta blockers block these receptors. They stop specific organs in the body (depending on the beta blocker used) from accepting adrenaline.

Originally beta blockers such as Propranolol (Inderal) were developed for people with heart problems. Taking them helps the heart to do less work in general and prevents it being over-worked in times of stress, which can be vital for people with a weak heart or recovering from a heart attack. Now, because of this action on the heart, beta blockers have become widely prescribed for anxiety problems.

One of the main symptoms of anxiety is a speeding heart, which is part of the fight-or-flight response. In times of danger our body produces adrenaline to make the heart beat faster to get blood and oxygen (fuel) to our major muscles (arms, chest and legs) more quickly to enable us to fight or flee. Stopping the heart from beating faster makes us feel calmer.

Taking beta blockers also makes us feel less shaky since the energy boost to our muscles (which makes us feel 'jittery' and 'on-edge') doesn't happen without a fast heartbeat.

With these obvious benefits, it may seem that beta blockers are the ideal solution for anxiety. But it's not as simple as this.

Although they aren't naturally physically addictive (as tranquillizers are) they can soon become psychologically addictive and we quickly come to feel that we cannot do anything before taking a tablet.

Also, beta blockers only block the adrenaline – they don't stop it. And the question remains as to what happens to the adrenaline our body produces.

Perhaps more importantly, long-term usage of beta blockers can alter the natural function of the heart and stopping this medication without medical supervision can be very dangerous. This may be a necessary risk if the alternative is a heart attack... but to deal with anxiety?

It is important to realise that beta blockers are not a cure for anxiety problems. They dampen some of the symptoms but do not deal with the underlying reason for the anxiety. Also, there are many other side effects to consider such as: weight gain, depression, tiredness, impotence or loss of libido, blurred vision and sleep disturbance.

As a temporary relief for dealing with stressful events, the short-term usage of beta blockers may be beneficial. But in using beta blockers long-term to deal with anxiety problems… the risks may outweigh the benefits.

* * *

"I have a mental illness caused by something going wrong in my brain and only medication can help."

What we think, we become.

Current ideas and beliefs about generalized anxiety disorder, OCD, social phobia, PTSD, panic disorder and depression consign millions of people to a lifetime of suffering, feeling helpless and without hope, simply enduring these problems whilst finding bits of relief through medication.

These problems take many years to develop fully and the starting point is often anxiety, increased anxiety over an extended period of time. Now it seems that just the mention of the 'a' word automatically leads us down the path of disorders, mental illness and medication. Yet when we look at anxiety through the lens of human evolution and survival a very different picture emerges. It's not one of dis-order but order, a totally logical and predictable human response in reaction to many life experiences.

Increased anxiety is not an illness but the result of learning and conditioning, and once we understand how this happens we are in a far stronger position to deal with it.

...

PART II

NATURAL ANXIETY

...

3

Understanding Anxiety
and How it Works

IMAGINE YOU'RE LYING on a beach. It's a beautiful day, the sun is shining and there is a gentle breeze wafting over your body. Sounds of nature fill the air as you chat and laugh with family and friends. You are surrounded by people that you love and respect and they love and respect you. You feel lovely and warm, calm, contented and happy, totally relaxed, anxiety-free.

Now imagine a very different scene. It's the dead of night and you are walking alone down a dimly lit alley. There are doorways on either side – who knows what's hiding in them, waiting to pounce?

You are scared and all your senses are heightened. Your sight and hearing have become more sensitive, able to pinpoint the slightest movement or sound. Your breathing and heartbeat have become more rapid, you feel light-headed and dizzy and have an overwhelming desire to go to the toilet or throw up. Your limbs feel shaky and your whole body is now charged with energy, full of anxiety, ready to fight or flee, possibly for your life.

These two scenes represent either end of the anxiety scale. In the first we feel warm, secure and safe; we are fully relaxed. In the second we are really anxious, highly alert and scared. We are prepared for danger.

* * *

Anxiety is a survival instinct that has evolved over millions of years in order to protect us from getting hurt. It is a series of reflexes and responses involving thoughts and feelings that affect our mind and body as we become prepared to avoid or deal with dangerous situations.

Every single person on the planet has anxiety. It's an essential part of human make up designed to keep us alive and it does this in two main ways:-

Firstly, it helps prepare our body for action, making us more alert, ready to fight or flee from any danger or threat to our survival. Often referred to as 'the fight-or-flight response', this is responsible for the direct physical sensations (such as rapid heartbeat, fast breathing, being jittery and on-edge, trembling etc.) that we feel when we are anxious. In real, imminent danger we can go from being totally relaxed to extremely anxious in an instant, which is panic.

Initiated by the release of adrenaline from the adrenal gland the moment we perceive any danger, this fight-or-flight response explains most all of the physical anxiety and panic symptoms that we experience. Some of the symptoms may be enhanced by thoughts, for example: a dry throat, with subsequent perceived difficulty when swallowing, may be built up into feeling we are choking, but in essence everything that is happening to our body is a result of it being physically prepared for action.

Much of this preparation involves the re-directing of resources to the major muscle groups (legs/arms/chest) to provide them with an energy boost for action and enable us, ultimately, to fight or flee:-

- Our *breathing becomes more rapid* to get more oxygen (fuel) for these muscles into the blood.
- Our *heartbeat speeds up* to get this freshly oxygenated blood to the muscles more quickly.
- Blood is diverted from the brain (making us *light-headed* and *dizzy*) and from the stomach (causing '*butterflies*').
- Energy cannot be wasted processing any half-digested food in our system so we need to get rid of it quickly – either through the mouth (*feelings of nausea*) or the other end (*wanting to go to the toilet*).
- Other 'energy-wasting' systems (unnecessary in time of danger) are shut down eg. saliva production, giving us a *dry mouth* and *difficulty swallowing*.
- We *sweat more* to cool down all this energy production.
- The energy boost to the muscles makes them feel '*jumpy*' / '*jittery*' / '*jelly-like*'/ '*on edge*' ready for action.

These physical symptoms of anxiety form the basis of problems such as general nervousness, social phobias (in fact, almost all phobias) and panic disorder.

*

Secondly, anxiety causes us to plan ahead for any potential dangers and how we might deal with them. We also imagine any painful consequences. This is an excellent survival strategy (it's better to deal with a danger or avoid it before we get into the situation) but an unfortunate effect of this is that we can get nervous and anxious just thinking about certain situations.

A main ingredient in the cause of certain anxiety disorders, this function is related to symptoms such as persistent negative thoughts and excessive worrying.

* * *

The physical and mental aspects of anxiety affect us so strongly ("What is wrong with me?") that it may be wise to examine them in more detail. Let's look into them a little deeper to find out what is happening and why, and in doing so remove some of the mystery that surrounds them:-

Palpitations

A speeding heart is one of the defining symptoms of anxiety. We cannot be anxious with a calm, slow-beating heart.

To most people, heart palpitations mean strong, fast heartbeats and a faster pulse – something we can easily associate with anxiety and panic. However, palpitations also refer to missed or skipped beats.

For the most part, heart palpitations are harmless but it is very important to have any symptoms checked by a medical professional to rule out physical causes that may be serious.

Palpitations may be warning signs for heart disease, an over-active thyroid or due to certain prescription medications – problems that require medical attention. A doctor should be called immediately for palpitations that also involve chest pain, loss of consciousness or shortness of breath.

Non-serious heart palpitations often occur due to external things that we take such as caffeine, nicotine and illegal drugs or may result from vigorous exercise. These are a direct result of something we take or do, are usually less frequent and don't indicate anything is physically wrong.

Another category of palpitations, whilst not serious in the sense of indicating physical illness, generally occur more frequently, involve both speeding heart and missed beats and reflect an underlying problem that needs attention. These are the heart palpitations caused by anxiety and panic.

Every year in the United States and the United Kingdom tens of thousands of people visit hospital emergency wards fearing they are having a heart attack… only to discover they were having an anxiety or panic attack. The strong, rapid heartbeat really did make them fear the worst.

Why does our heart speed up so?

Anxiety and panic prepare us to deal with danger, either to fight or run away (the 'fight-or-flight' response). The heart beats faster to pump oxygen (fuel) more quickly to the major muscle groups (arms, legs, chest) to provide them with an energy boost for fighting or fleeing. The greater the danger, the quicker we need energy to take action so the faster the heart pumps.

With long-term anxiety and stress our heart generally beats faster than normal at rest and it doesn't take much for it to increase into the first stages of panic (a harder, faster beat), which we notice as heart palpitations.

This also explains the 'skipped beats' phenomenon. A heart that is continuously beating faster than normal will occasionally miss a beat in order to correct the pace.

Breathing Too Fast

In an effort to provide the extra oxygen (fuel) that our muscles need to take immediate action we breathe faster to take in more air.

In a truly dangerous situation this is exactly what we need – extra oxygen to keep our muscles supplied as we use it up rapidly in working them hard to fight or flee.

However, if we are breathing faster, drawing more oxygen into our blood, but not using it quickly (fighting or fleeing) – that is we are anxious but not taking any physical action – then our self-protective behaviour actually makes things worse for it disrupts the normal oxygen(O_2)-carbon dioxide(CO_2) balance in the blood.

In the normal breathing cycle we take in O_2 and expel CO_2. During exercise we take in O_2 faster and expel CO_2 faster as needed. However, breathing faster without any corresponding increase in action leads to a build up of oxygen in the bloodstream, which has negative effects.

When we are breathing too fast (hyperventilating) it can feel as if there is not enough oxygen (which makes us more panicky). However, the reverse is true – we actually have too much oxygen. For although carbon dioxide is a waste gas that we breathe out, we need a certain amount of it in our bloodstream to be able to use up the oxygen we have. When we hyperventilate we end up with an excess of oxygen that we cannot actually use. Hence it can feel like we don't have enough oxygen.

This is why people who are hyperventilating are often told to breathe into paper bags – to breathe in the CO_2 they are breathing out, which redresses the O_2-CO_2 balance. It also shows us why exercise and deep breathing (diaphragmatic breathing) can help alleviate anxiety. We'll talk more about these later.

Excessive Sweating

Sweating too much (from the armpits, hands and often the face) is a very common anxiety symptom.

Sweating excessively usually happens during physical exertion (such as exercise) or when we are too hot. It's the body's way of helping us to cool down. The warm sweat reaches the body surface where it evaporates, taking heat away from the body.

We all know that we sweat during vigorous exercise and in high temperatures, but why do we sweat due to anxiety and panic?

The fight-or-flight response is initiated by adrenaline, which increases our body's metabolism to prepare us for action. This increase in metabolism produces heat.

To counteract this, adrenaline also stimulates the sweat glands to cool down any heat produced so even small amounts of anxiety may cause us to sweat more. Many people experience 'sweaty palms' even though they are only mildly anxious.

Feeling Nauseous / Needing the Toilet

It takes many hours and numerous body resources to extract the nutrients and process the waste from any food that we have eaten – time and resources we can't spare in an emergency.

As such, any half-digested food needs to be got rid of quickly, either from the mouth or the other end. It probably depends on where the food is sitting in our system (the top half or bottom half) as to which way is possible to expel it.

This fight-or-flight response also explains why we often have no appetite or feel sick at the thought of food when we are anxious.

Dizziness and Feeling Faint

Dizziness can have a number of physical causes such as ear infections, diabetes and circulation problems so it is very important to have any recurring dizziness checked out by a doctor.

When no physical causes are present it is highly likely that bouts of dizziness are due to anxiety. When we are anxious or panicky many of us feel light-headed and dizzy. We often become confused and find it difficult to think straight or concentrate. Some people think they are about to faint... but why?

In part, once again, it boils down to that diversion of resources to those things we need to survive. Blood is diverted form the higher regions of our brain to the areas we need most in the moment, such as vision and hearing. We don't need time to think, just time to be ultra aware and act. If we had to think about jumping out of the way of a speeding car it would be too late.

Hearing and vision become more acute when we are anxious and it's interesting to note that one of the side effects of many beta blockers (which essentially prevent adrenaline from doing it's job) is blurred vision.

Too much oxygen in the bloodstream (related to the O_2-CO_2 balance we covered earlier) can also make us feel light-headed and dizzy.

Trembling and Shakiness

Going back to that dimly lit alley... as we approach the dark doorways, in which anything could be hiding, we feel 'jittery' and shaky. Our muscles are trembling;

they are primed and ready to spring into action in a split second. Adrenaline has flooded our system to energize us, which make us feel shaky.

Shakiness (or trembling) is extremely common and is one sure fire way to tell when someone is anxious. Many people who appear outwardly calm often feel shaky inside when anxiety strikes.

On a popular TV quiz show, where the contestants answer questions and can double their winnings up to a million, the quizmaster has said to many contestants, words to the effect, "You look remarkably calm". In nearly every instance, the reply has been the same – "On the outside yes, but inside I'm shaking like a leaf."

*

The above represent the physical aspects of anxiety. The sensations (symptoms) that we experience and the strength of these sensations vary from person to person.

Some people sweat more, others tremble whilst for many the main focus is palpitations.

It's important to realise that when we focus on one particular symptom and start to worry about it, this causes more anxiety and actually increases the problem.

With symptoms such as sweating and shaking where our 'weakness' is clearly visible to others it is remarkably easy to fall into a cycle of worrying about the problem which increases anxiety, which increases the problem, which increases the worrying and so on.

Worrying

We all worry about bad things that could happen, to some extent. It's usually about things we cannot fully control such as falling ill, accidents happening, losing our job, financial troubles and being attacked.

Worrying causes us to consider these things and what the consequences may be. It guides us into taking pre-emptive action to avoid them. This level of worry is normal and in a sense it may be better described as planning.

Planning reflects attempts to be in control. Armies plan and re-plan for possible future events in order to have some idea of what to do if they arise. To man, planning does indeed instil a sense of knowledge and competence in the face of unforeseen events.

An appropriate amount of planning and worrying is adaptive and conducive to survival... excessive worry is not.

Excessive worrying results when our planning doesn't make us feel any more secure and it doesn't allay our anxiety. It's one of the main symptoms of generalized anxiety disorder.

Here, when our anxiety is great, we believe that we are anxious (prepared) because something bad is going to happen – but what? We don't know, so we imagine various bad things that could happen and start planning to avoid them. But the planning is not real control; it doesn't help the future and it doesn't make us feel any better or safer. It is illusory, only secondary control, and it doesn't work. So we plan more, feel worse and plan more.

Now we are no longer planning carefully about what to do, just worrying excessively about a myriad of things that could happen. And we cannot stop it because we feel it *is* the answer. We believe it is the way to get control and stop potential bad things from happening.

* * *

When looking at anxiety and its role as a 'preparer' and 'protector' there are two more things we need to consider. One, that we have already mentioned, is panic and the other is nervousness.

Nervousness, Anxiety and Panic

"I feel nervous." "I feel anxious." Is there any real difference between these two sentiments?

Am I nervous before a first date or am I anxious? And what is happening when my heart is beating rapidly, I'm breathing heavily and have uncontrollable thoughts of impending doom – is it an anxiety attack or a panic attack?

Nervousness, anxiety and panic lie on a continuum.

NERVOUSNESS ←→ ANXIETY ←→ PANIC

They are all based on survival instincts and the fight-or-flight response and are fundamentally the same, differing only in intensity and speed of onset.

Through the same bodily processes we can experience mild, vague feelings of unease and apprehension, being slightly nervous about some distant danger, or be so panic-stricken about an imminent threat that all we can do is flee.

Perhaps this is best illustrated using the following example:-

Take the man who is scared of public speaking that has to make a speech at his friend's wedding in a few weeks time...

- Weeks away, just thinking about the wedding will make him nervous. Probably only slightly for everything is still some time away.

- Days away from the event he'll be starting to get extremely anxious just thinking about it. The nervousness grows into anxiety, which gets stronger and stronger as the day of the speech draws near.

- The morning of the wedding he is now panic-stricken, terrified about making the speech – so much so that he gets drunk enough to face it or makes excuses to get out of it and avoids doing it altogether.

It may be that the mind takes the lead during an anxiety attack whereas it's the body in a panic attack. However, in both cases the dominating role is often supplemented, altered or enhanced by the other and it's always self-protection that sets things off.

Fear drives all anxiety, the instinctive response to the threat of being hurt. Dangerous situations (or the thought of them) cause reactions in our body and mind and it's these reactions as much as the threat itself that guide our behaviour. We don't have to stand up close to a lion and see its teeth and claws to be afraid. One far off in the distance can cause enough anxiousness in our mind and body to keep us well away from it.

Some fears are programmed into us for survival. It probably didn't take too many attacks by wild animals on our distant ancestors for them to realise the danger and learn to avoid such animals or be prepared when facing them. An inner 'preparedness' for such dangers increases the chances of survival for the species. Fears programmed for survival include the following four categories:-

- Potentially dangerous animals, insects and people.
- Naturally dangerous environments such as heights and darkness.
- Dangerous situations. For example, being trapped in confined spaces.
- Infection and disease / blood and injury.

Other fears we learn. And some of these may be weird and wonderful or seem trivial yet at the heart of them all remains the underlying fear of injury or death and the ultimate goal of self-protection and survival.

Take, for instance, Coulrophobia: the fear of clowns. With clowns, we cannot tell in their faces their true intention towards us – that painted-on smile could mask mal-intent. It takes away our sense of control since we cannot judge for our self whether they are truly friendly or mean us harm. Rooted in early man's fear of strangers and possible attack this fear has been adapted by learning.

But how do we learn fears?

One way is by observing others. Watching someone being hurt by an object or situation quickly teaches us that such objects or situations are dangerous and to be wary of them. But the strongest way to learn to fear something is through personal experience and this happens by a process known as conditioning.

Conditioning

Through conditioning, repeated exposure to situations (and importantly, things associated with them) can elicit responses in our body that become 'ingrained' in us. We become 'programmed' to react in certain ways to certain things.

In a classic experiment performed in the early 1900's, the forerunner of nearly all experiments on conditioning,

Ivan Pavlov, a Russian physiologist, demonstrated how this works.

Hungry dogs were presented with food and they would salivate, a natural response elicited by the smell of the food. Then a light would be turned on just before the food was presented. This was repeated a number of times and eventually the light would be turned on without any food being presented to the dogs; they would salivate at the light alone.

Light does not induce salivation in dogs, food does. The light had become associated with the food and now it could make the dogs salivate on its own. Here we see a real example of bodily responses based on associations and, in humans, fear by association forms the basis of many anxiety problems.

Of course, the properties of the light itself did not cause the salivation; it was the connection to what was coming next (the food). Perceptions of what is going to happen next, and 'what could happen', underlie all fears. With the lion example earlier, we don't have to go any closer to it for we know what could happen.

Nowhere is the fear of 'what could happen' seen more explicitly than in generalized anxiety disorder where excessive worrying over what might happen defines the disorder.

Look at conditioning in this way: if every time you walked through a blue door someone punched you in the face, it wouldn't take very long for you to become really scared of blue doors and start avoiding them.

Similarly, it's not difficult to imagine how a teenager that isn't the tallest person, isn't the best looking nor the brightest, who is continually teased and made fun of (with academic results and sports results on public display), may start to feel so bad and out of control over many aspects of school life that school itself becomes the object of fear.

Conditioning, rooted in basic survival fears, underpins many anxiety problems today but before we explore this in greater detail there is one property of anxiety it is essential to understand. That is: why anxiety gets worse.

It's tempting, and it fits in with our feelings and the current worldview, to attribute this to an awful mental illness that nobody can really understand or cure. But it isn't – it's just how anxiety works.

Returning to our fear of blue doors... If we become scared of blue doors and start avoiding them regularly, over time something strange (but predictable) starts to happen. We begin to fear more doors; those that aren't actually blue but may be similar. Grey doors, green doors, similar shaped doors, indeed a whole myriad of doors now begin to make us afraid (cause anxiety) and we start to avoid these too.

This is seen in all anxiety disorders where the initial fear starts to spread. In generalized anxiety disorder, we start to worry about more and more; in OCD, the rituals become longer and more intricate; in social phobia, the fear spreads to more and more social situations.

It's not about any illness getting worse but purely down to anxiety trying to protect us. Basically, if something is making us fearful and we don't resolve it we will start to become scared of similar things (objects or situations) on the assumption that these could also hurt us.

This is known in psychology as 'generalisation' (or the generalisation of fears) and once again there is classic research to demonstrate it.

In an ethically and morally questionable experiment in the 1920's, an infant, 'little Albert', who was initially unafraid of a rat, was made to fear the rat through classical conditioning. A loud noise was made near the child whenever the rat was introduced. The child soon developed a very strong fear of the rat and this fear eventually extended to furry toys. Little Albert became afraid of the rat and anything that was even vaguely like the rat.

Although critics have questioned the results of this experiment, we know that this does happen for adults can become scared of photographs. Indeed it is fairly common for severe arachnophobics to be petrified of mere pictures of spiders.

* * *

Anxiety, our very own personal survival instinct, involves a series of reflexes, responses and reactions that have developed over millions of years in order to save us from injury or worse. It's innate, programmed into us; we don't have to consciously think about protecting our self – anxiety does it for us.

Rooted in fears over survival and the fight-or-flight response, the preparation and energization of our body can be seen at an early age: observe the small child 'jumping' when startled at being caught out in some secretive act.

In the past, threat and danger were everywhere and for many people life really was a battle to survive. Anxiety and the fight-or-flight response served our ancestors well, but the world we live in today is very different from the one we inhabited thousands of years ago.

...

4

Anxious Times

IT CANNOT BE SAID often enough: everyone has anxiety, a survival instinct that's evolved over millions of years, to help protect us from being hurt. It prepares us to deal with anything that may harm us by avoiding it, fighting or running away. To fight or flee, the fight-or-flight response – it is this that we come to associate with being scared.

In the past, dangerous things that could harm us (and made us scared) included the likes of wild animals, poisonous snakes and insects, strangers, heights and confined spaces. Being confronted by any of these could have been life threatening.

In the modern world we no longer face the direct threats of our ancestors. They still exist of course (wild animals, dangerous strangers etc.) and could potentially kill us in certain circumstances, but they don't impact our lives as they did hundreds of years ago.

Today, the things that make us feel scared are more subtle and vague. Their effects build up slowly over time and include such things as:-

- Conflict with family members
- Conflict with peers and partners in relationships
- Trouble with work colleagues or the job itself
- Money, bills and fear of debt
- Health, diet and the fear of illness
- Violence in the world as reported daily in the news

All the above can make us feel bad, unhappy and miserable for a very long time. They involve threat and a lack of control and start to fill us with insecurity.

As we go through life there are many situations and circumstances that involve unpleasant experiences and can lead to inner feelings of weakness and vulnerability. Let's take a closer look at some of the significant ones:-

In The Family

Family conflict is one sure fire way to instil deep feelings of insecurity in a child as they grow.

There has been much debate and research around the influence of parents on a person's emotional health. Parents have gone from being fully responsible or having no responsibility at all, to a middle ground where other things such as peers, school, society and the media play a major part. And these things do play a part, a very important part (and we'll come to them later) but nothing affects us quite like our parents. Their genes are our genes and from the day we are born we are shaped by their beliefs, attitudes and behaviours; we are moulded by their hopes and fears, and the way they make us feel often sets the foundation for how we feel about our self for much of our life.

There are two very common family conflict situations involving our parents that invariably lead to massive feelings of insecurity. These are parental conflict and parental criticism.

Parental Conflict

"The most important thing a father can do for his children is to love their mother."

...Henry Ward Beecher (1813–1887)

Perhaps a truer word has never been spoken. When our parents argue we feel awful, simple as that.

Fighting parents pose a threat to a child's sense of safety. Their fighting instils feelings of insecurity, worry and self-doubt and it doesn't take a great leap in faith or imagination to see how regular and extreme arguing between parents can leave a child in an almost constant state of distress. It makes them feel bad and that there is nothing they can do about it – two of the essential elements for anxiety.

Parental Criticism

Constructive criticism, given and received correctly, can be extremely beneficial. But there are no benefits from destructive criticism. It destroys children; it can destroy anyone.

Destructive personal criticism is an attack and it's not just the words used. Being told that we are *'stupid'* or *'useless'*, that *'we can't do anything right'*, that *'we always fail'* and *'will never amount to anything'* or that we are *'pathetic'*, *'fat'*, *'lazy'* or *'ignorant'* is bad enough but it doesn't end there. It is the manner in which such things are said to us that damages the most.

To be called *'stupid'* by someone jokingly with a smile is not the same as being called *'stupid'* by someone who is angry and exuding hatred and disgust.

Unfortunately, some parents do criticise their children in such a way – harsh words said in a harsh manner. And when this happens frequently it can't help but cause deep insecurity and self-doubt.

As a young child, we don't have the acquired brain development, experience and knowledge to work things out for our self so we build our self-estimate solely on the appraisal of others and how they react to us – when these appraisals come from our parents we don't doubt them.

Also, with constant criticism, be it direct or implied, we can never do well enough and eventually we come to think that it is actually us, our self, our very being that is not good enough.

There is no question as to the role of parents regarding the emotional health of their children. They give us life and keep us alive. They feed us, clothe us and provide shelter. They protect us and they hurt us. They make us feel good and they make us feel bad. Indeed, almost all of the rewards and punishments that a child receives are mediated by the parents.

But it's not just our parents. Conflict with other family members often leads to those inner feelings of insecurity that awakens our anxiety. Constant bullying by spouses, siblings, or step-parents can have a profound effect, and long-standing arguments and rifts between extended family members also have a role to play.

And it's not only direct conflict situations that leave us feeling bad and without control. Loss of a parent, divorce, money problems, expectations and pressures to achieve and many more situations can do the same.

Suffice to say that, within the context of the family, there are many situations and circumstances that can make us feel bad for a very long time and lead us to conclude that there is nothing we can do about it – a vulnerability that our survival instinct just cannot allow.

Peers, Groups and Belonging

Throughout life our friends and peers hold a strong influence over us. Children talk like their peers (often inventing new words), dress like their peers and act like them.

We look to our peers for guidance on how to function in society and they help shape our identity. Soon we begin to associate personal qualities with acceptance and rejection. Desirable qualities often include strength, good looks and fitness for boys, and being slim and pretty for girls. This is nature and survival at play, nothing else.

Even at an early age, social acceptance is a must. Being accepted by the group feels good, being rejected feels bad and we soon come to realise how we should 'be' and how to act in order to be liked and accepted.

Groups can promote a sense of belonging and identity and increase our self-esteem through feelings of being needed.

Conversely, to not belong is to be alone and have to defend oneself. Most animals form groups to survive; a lone wildebeest is easy prey while a group of one hundred wildebeest dramatically increases the odds of an individual's survival. We'll do almost anything to prevent being cast out from the group and many 'follow like sheep' rather than go against the majority and be seen to be different. Numerous studies have shown that a person will give a knowingly wrong answer in agreement with other wrong answers rather than stand out from the crowd by giving the correct answer.

Regarding peers and groups: to not be accepted or liked or to not 'fit in' can cause massive insecurity for it involves perhaps the greatest underlying fear that we all have: the fear of rejection.

For with rejection comes the threat of being cast out and left on our own... alone, unable to survive.

School and the Workplace

School and the workplace provide a very public display of our position in life. Great if you're at the top but not so good if you're at the bottom.

For many, going to school is like facing a phobia every day. We head to school knowing that we are going to be bullied again and knowing that we cannot do anything about it. We go to school knowing that we will be expected to perform and not only are we forced to perform, but also the result of our performance will be seen by all. Every test is an opportunity to show that we are not good enough, another opportunity to let our parents and our teachers down... to let our self down.

Is it any wonder that some children, feeling bad and insecure inside, develop phobias of going to school where they are made to feel even more insecure?

Similarly, in the workplace our talents and abilities (or lack of) are pretty much common knowledge.

In school and in the workplace, to have our weakness on public display can only add to the fear of rejection.

School and work provide the environment for one of the greatest causes of anxiety (and depression) problems there is. It's a situation in which we can be in (or feel as though we are in) real, imminent physical danger and it has destroyed countless lives. It is... being bullied.

Bullying

Of course this doesn't only take place at school or work. One of the things we looked at earlier represents one of the worst kinds of bullying: harsh, destructive parental criticism.

Bullying involves various threats and dangers. We may feel unworthy of love (and be rejected) when it's from our parents or partner; fear losing our livelihood (hence food and shelter) if our boss is the bully; or be in actual physical danger from a fellow pupil.

When we are bullied we are victimised, under attack incessantly and helpless. There is often very little we can do to protect our self or prevent attack from people, or groups of people, that are more powerful than us. It leads to those feelings of helplessness and hopelessness that characterise severe anxiety and depression. Often we have no power to change the situation and can only suffer it. We are under great threat and have no control.

The things we have looked at so far generally involve personal interactions with others and affect us on a more direct level. Home, school and the workplace provide the environment for these interactions to take place, however there are two more things, the broader environment if you like, that we need to consider. These are society and religion. Although less direct, the effect that these two things have on our sense of well-being and security can be profound.

Society

Society represents a struggle against true nature for almost everyone. The rules, regulations and laws temper evolutionary survival instincts and instil a conformity that holds populations together. (Most sane people will renounce murder, rape and genocide despite them being potentially beneficial for the progression of our genes.) Conflict between instincts and the rules of society exists in all of us.

An undercurrent of insecurity runs through all of our lives since most of the rules and regulations are based on fear. We fear being punished or cast out from the main group (imprisoned) if we do wrong and any real fears we may have over being attacked personally or about society being attacked are often overplayed by leaders to impose control. Indeed, we have very little real control at all since the government, the church, employers and educational systems direct much of our lives.

Albeit small and perhaps of greater influence to some people than others, the society in which we live creates underlying insecurities relating to *'how to be'* and *'what to do'* in order to fit in. Fears over the need to belong in groups and possible rejection enslave us once again. But it's less direct and the effect of society's rules and regulations on many of us may be relatively small (depending on the society). However there is another element to society, particularly modern-day Western society, that increases this effect dramatically and we'll look at this shortly.

Religion

Like society, religion pervades our very existence, dictating standards and ideals of beliefs and behaviour in order to promote conformity.

In all religions we have to be 'good' in some way. We have to behave in strictly defined ways (different ways for different religions) in order to please the Lord so that we can go to Heaven rather than Hell. And generally we do... we behave in ways we are told to rather than ways that are true to our self.

Religion helps to keep society together (and is also responsible for the death of untold numbers through war) but it demands conformity based on the fear of retribution, and what a retribution – punishment by God! If we don't conform to the standards set out in our religion, the threat of punishment by God can induce anxiety and fear in an instant.

Today, how many people struggle against the tide of insecurity over not being 'a good enough Christian' or 'a good enough Catholic' or 'a good enough Muslim'?

And what of the child brought up in a very strict religious household, under the constant threat of being punished by God for any wrongdoing? Here, sadly, a life ruled by OCD and rituals is almost inevitable.

*

The family, society, religion, school and the workplace have been around in one form or another for centuries.

The family group provides us with love, nurture and support to enable us to survive, grow and thrive. School and the workplace give us the opportunity to learn and explore and to develop new talents and skills. They also provide us with the opportunity to achieve and create.

Society bonds the group together and helps to keep us safe, as does religion to some degree. For many, belief in God gets them through the hard times in life.

These environments can be extremely positive for many people but this book is not about that. It's about the development of fear and anxiety and how these can be conditioned into us in our daily lives.

Throughout life we are often drawn into situations that make us feel scared, weak and vulnerable. When these situations persist or get worse (or the number of situations increases) we start to feel insecure more often. Eventually anxiety, our self-protection system, kicks in. This may be mild at first, usually in the form of increased nervousness or some anxiety-related symptom may appear. We may notice that we are more shaky, sweating more, experiencing frequent heart palpitations, tightness across the chest or feeling nauseous often. Any symptom related to anxiety can develop and worrying about these symptoms only makes them worse for it increases our general anxiety.

If the situation remains unresolved we can become more and more anxious (with various anxiety symptoms getting worse) for seemingly no apparent reason.

This increased anxiousness reflects our mind and body warning us that something is not right in our life, something is making us insecure and we need to stop it or get away from it. Anxiety is trying to protect us.

Nervousness, anxiety and panic fade away once the danger is over. Once we've outrun that wild animal or fought off an attacker, calmness returns when we are safe. Similarly, if we think about a potentially dangerous situation in advance, and avoid it, our anxiety subsides once the threat is removed.

It's not difficult to see then, that in situations where the threat is not removed but comes back regularly to hurt us, that anxiety will not completely go away. Why would it? We are still in potential danger and may need to fight or flee at any time.

With constant threat, an undercurrent of anxiety flows through us; we are always slightly prepared, alert and ready for action. We become more tense, like a coiled spring, and over time the increase in our resting heart-beat rate confirms this.

We now live in a state of higher physiological arousal than those whose self-protective instincts aren't required to such an extent on a daily basis.

We've been conditioned to be afraid. And it involves a vague, background anxiety since there is no direct cause, no immediate threat, which we can fight or flee.

Over time, if not resolved, our fear usually grows stronger as it evolves to cover more and more situations through generalisation.

This is how anxiety increases: insidiously, without apparent reason and it explains how many people live their lives today – 'on-edge' for much of the time.

The amount of anxiety that we eventually come to live with depends largely on the number and strength of the feelings of weakness, insecurity and vulnerability that we have experienced.

But the story doesn't end there.

*

"You look remarkably calm."
"Yes, but inside I'm shaking like a leaf."

Sitting there, on a televised quiz show in front of millions of viewers, with a chance of giving the wrong answer... who wouldn't be scared?

These contestants are very anxious, and rightly so, since they are in a frightening situation. Yet they are not overwhelmed by their anxiety for they attribute it all to the situation, and as such it can be very unpleasant but still controllable. (Although unlikely to happen, they can walk away (flee) at any time.)

Anxiety becomes a real problem when it ceases to be about the situation and becomes *something about our self*.

Something About Us

A charging animal, an attacker, a dimly lit alley – in all of these cases there is a good reason to be anxious.

Here, the anxiety has a direct cause, a real threat, and we can do something about that threat. We can avoid it, fight our way out of it or flee from it. We do have some control.

However, when anxiety increases insidiously over time, the result of many instances of feeling vulnerable, things are very different. There is no direct reason for it, which makes our anxiety seem to come from nowhere and we have no control over it since avoidance, fighting or fleeing aren't real options.

To live like this (anxious without reason or control) also isn't an option. Our mind won't allow us to remain in such a state for long. We have to find the reason for our anxiety so that we can do something about it.

Eventually, through further experience and learning we come to find the reason for our increased anxiety. It is because of us, our self. We have anxiety because we are in some way *'not good enough'*, *'bad'* or *'wrong'*.

Depending on many factors, it can take years to reach this conclusion (as seen in many anxiety disorders and severe depression problems) or it may never be reached at all if we find ways to behave or live that compensate for our anxiety.

However there are two things, pertinent to modern-day Western society, that make it far easier (and quicker) to come to the conclusion that we have anxiety because there is something wrong with us.

The first one bears great responsibility for a dramatic increase in serious anxiety and depression problems worldwide and the second one has had such an explosive effect on society that these problems have skyrocketed to almost epidemic proportions. They are, respectively, the media and social media.

Social Animals

We need others. Alone, we cannot thrive and we can't make babies for the species to survive.

Human beings are social animals from the moment they are born. An infant doesn't have to learn how to cry, it is a pre-programmed survival behaviour to attract others who can provide security and care.

The modern family has evolved from the tribes of our ancestors, with extended families reflecting attempts to keep as many members of the unit as safe as possible. We live as we have always lived, in groups, and we depend on our ability to cooperate with others for survival. Whether it's finding food, building shelter, warding off predators or bringing up children, the pooling of resources serves to enhance mutual survival. This is why we all have a desperate need to be accepted and consequently a deep-seated fear of rejection.

However, alongside the need for personal protection and survival through the acceptance by others, flows another need: the need to progress our genes.

Within the group, we are driven to establish some recognition, some success and status to help us develop relationships and gain a 'successful' mate in order to produce 'better' offspring. The more recognition and success we achieve, the more status we gain in the group and this effectively enhances the survival chances of any children we may have.

Competition drives all species; it promotes the production of 'stronger and fitter' offspring so we are designed to compete. Winning feels good. In fact it feels very good, so much so that some people will do almost anything to win, to achieve success and survive better. The nature of things is such that competition between males usually involves size, strength and power while competition between females usually involves beauty and attraction.

In order to drive this competition, just as winning feels good, losing and failure feel bad. Indeed, they feel so awful that we never want to feel this way. Cortisol (a hormone released in times of stress) courses through our bloodstream, feel-good chemicals ebb away leaving us extremely tired and we feel sick to the stomach. This serves as a powerful reminder not to make the same mistake again. A similar reaction occurs with 'losing face' where we don't want to fail and be seen to fail, and lose position within the group.

[Note that this forms the basis of why we get anxious over things like tests, interviews, first dates and public speaking. In these situations we don't want to be seen as weak or a failure and possibly be rejected because of it. (To further protect us from rejection, it really is painful – brain-imaging work has shown that the brain's response to pain and rejection is quite similar).

In the examples above (with the exception of public speaking), any possible rejection that we may face is relatively mild. It is localised (situation based) and the potential pain it may cause is correspondingly small. Thus the anxiety we experience is also relatively mild, and it usually leads to greater preparation to face the situation (smartening up our appearance, increasing our knowledge etc.) rather than avoidance.

Things are slightly different with public speaking. Here, our 'failure' may be seen by many people, hence the fear of it can be much greater. Indeed, fear of public speaking is the number one fear for many people.]

Just like the social norms for acceptance, our knowledge, and ultimately belief, about what constitutes success comes from social learning. We observe others and make comparisons. We compare our self to others.

When we live with an undercurrent of anxiety and insecurity we look for reasons to explain this and things that confirm it. This invariably leads to a blinkered focus on negative comparisons since these confirm how we feel. (The man, insecure about his height, who is 5 feet 8 inches tall, always compares himself to men who are 6 foot 2, never to those who are 5 foot 6).

Now we'll turn to the two things that have not only radically changed society's standards, ideals and norms but also present opportunities for us to compare our self unfavourably to others virtually everywhere we turn.

The Media

There are a number of ways that the media, in itself, can increase levels of underlying anxiety in populations of people.

The television sits in the corner, bombarding us with messages all day, every day. Newspapers and news programmes bring real examples of war, violence and disease directly into our living room. Much of the time, stories aren't deemed newsworthy at all if they are not bad or shocking in some way hence most of what we see is bad news.

This must have some effect, however small, on the underlying levels of anxiety that we all feel.

However, a much greater effect can be felt when the more social aspects of media are involved, particularly those that claim to portray daily life. Here, multiple magazines and TV shows brainwash us into believing what happy and successful people look like and how they behave.

But it is false.

Society's standards and norms are now distorted and exaggerated all to attract viewers. The more viewers, the more money can be made from advertising. And it is this recent phenomenon of the modern world that has inflicted great damage on the collective psyche of society and the emotional health of the individual.

With advertising, we are deliberately made to feel inadequate and that nothing we have is quite good enough. But we can feel better, indeed we can be perfect and have perfect lives, just like those attractive people we see in the adverts – if only we buy the product!

Thanks largely to advertising, society is now obsessed with body image and most adverts play on our deep instincts relating to attraction and procreation. We all have instinctual concepts of beauty (even infants) for it is seen as an indicator of health and good genes, and advertisers use this for profit. Combining winning and losing and possessing with attractiveness and beauty, a strong bond is forged in our mind between body image and success. One research study in 1999 reported a five-fold increase in the symptoms associated with eating disorders among Fijian girls (normally robust and happy about it) since the arrival of TV to Fiji in 1995.

But we don't really need research to appreciate this. Tell me, how is the 'big' girl, desperately unhappy about her weight, supposed to feel when she is surrounded by images of happy, smiling people, all of whom are thin?

The media not only reflects society but also drives it. Certain parts of the media set false standards and ideals within society and promote them so much that they become the new normal for many people. Today we are surrounded by unrealistic and unattainable standards to compete with... and fail.

The social aspects of the media, driven by advertising and the profit margin, have affected all of us in some way. Now there is another player on the scene. A more recent phenomenon, the effects of which have only really surfaced in the last five to ten years. This focuses solely on the social side of things and is, of course, social media.

Social Media

Looks, body, clothes, wealth. Partners, school grades, lifestyle, health. Now we are able to compare our self to anyone, for any reason, whenever we want. Just a quick glance down to the palm of our hand and a few taps of the forefinger is all it takes to confirm that we are not good enough.

The little device that fits snuggly into the palm of our hand really does have a lot to answer for. Not only can it be used to harm our self on a regular basis but it also provides an ever-present opportunity for others to hurt us.

Today our kids don't even have to leave the house to be bullied and bullying via social media has destroyed the lives of many, many people.

Add to this the fact that our mistakes, inadequacies and weaknesses can be made public for the whole world to see and it paints a picture of increased threats and insecurity in today's society that didn't even exist a generation ago.

Of course, media in general (including the internet) and social media do have many good points. The media provides us with more ways to be informed, educated and entertained and social media allows us to keep in touch with family and friends, which reduces loneliness for many people.

The problem arises when profit becomes the driving force. Once big money enters the scene, any concern over damaging people quickly departs.

Often psychological tactics are used to attract and keep eyeballs on the television programme or the social media site in order to sell people's time to advertising.

Social media is designed to be addictive. The colours used, the smiley faces, the endless scroll – all of these serve to keep us on the site as long as possible.

'Likes' play on that basic human drive to compare (in order to see how successful we are, or not). Many 'likes' make us feel good and zero 'likes' make us feel bad. Our self worth becomes defined by how many 'likes' and 'followers' we have.

And we have no control over it. Every tap, click and swipe is analysed so that complicated algorithms can show us what other people want us to see. (Again, this is mostly driven by advertising).

Every time we receive a 'like' we get a little dopamine hit. Dopamine is a neurotransmitter (a chemical in the brain) associated with feeling good. Each time we get a 'like' we feel good and want more. It keeps us coming back. This can be very addictive (in the same way that gambling can be addictive) and there are reports of people suffering withdrawal symptoms when they try to give up social media. In fact, we can actually become anxious when we can't check our phone to see 'how we are doing' or what we are missing.

Think about this for a moment: something that is very addictive, that makes us anxious when we can't check it (and when we do check it, can make us feel bad in ways that play on our deepest fears) and is totally beyond our control…

The number of young people with (serious) anxiety and depression problems is spiralling out of control. Young people check their smart phones (social media) over 100 times a day.

The influence of the media, and particularly social media, can rapidly turn any underlying anxiety issues that we may have into something about us.

The ease with which we can compare our self to others in a multitude of ways dramatically influences how we start to feel about our self. Anxiety becomes inextricably linked to our self-esteem and self worth.

Any lack of ability or disability that we may have is magnified. The normal mixed-up feelings and emotions experienced during puberty and adolescence now exist in a society of warped social acceptance standards and there has been a massive rise in identity-crisis problems.

New advances within the media (and technology) are changing society dramatically. It's the young people that flock to embrace these advances. It's the young that are suffering the most.

*

The drive to survive and pass on genes is probably the ultimate goal of all life. To be rejected, cast out and alone threatens our very existence.

Anxiety becomes a real, serious problem when we believe it's due to 'something about us' for now it brings into play this deepest fear of all. And once the fear of rejection takes hold, it usually grows pretty rapidly for although it threatens our very survival, rejection is, in one sense, a vague threat, a background fear, one that exists through association, just like that fear of blue doors we talked about earlier. This not only makes it easier for conditioning to take place but also takes away much of our control.

We may be rejected, if…

We cannot control being rejected, only the 'if' part. And this usually boils down to something about us. (eg. we may be rejected if we are not good enough).

Without doubt, in the last few years, man has had to face many new sources of threat and insecurity that our ancestors couldn't have imagined. These sources prey on the greatest needs and fears we all have – the desperate need to be accepted and subsequent fear of rejection.

Now anxiety has a quick and easy way to shift from the original external cause to a more personal one.

However, before we move forward there is one more thing to add to the mix. It's the most recent development of all…

"I have anxiety, I have a mental illness."

We're not quite at this stage yet but we are getting there. Labelling anxiety and depression issues as mental illness immediately makes them *'something about us'*. It takes away all sense of control and leaves us helpless in many ways, just hoping for some miracle cure.

Thankfully there is a cure that doesn't rely on hope or miracles, but on insight and understanding – one that puts control firmly back in our own hands.

We're going to look at this in a moment, but first let's summarise *'anxious times'*.

In summary:

Anxiety, via the fight-or-flight response, served our distant ancestors well. It protected them from the real threats to life that were rife in days gone by.

Today, we have less to flee from; the threats we face are more subtle and vague. Actual physical danger is rare but these threats still make us feel insecure and vulnerable, so anxiety is very much involved.

We all experience conflict and insecurity within the family, society, education and work settings to some degree. Indeed, it may be this, as much as any inherent genetic trait, that determines the level of confidence with which we go through life.

General shyness and how nervous we get for tests, interviews and dates etc., comfort eating (along with the consequent yo-yo dieting) and a susceptibility to stress – all of these things are no doubt influenced by the amount of 'threat' that we've experienced in life and the level of background anxiety we carry around with us.

Things change when our anxiety starts to increase. It's often due to the long-term effect of high-threat situations (eg. parental criticism or bullying) or a combination of many different (smaller) threats, yet it seems to come from nowhere.

With no obvious direct cause, we begin to search for something to explain why this is happening to us. And finally, we discover the answer… it's to do with our self.

This realisation usually comes to us subconsciously through observing, comparing, further experiences and learning. And it often requires high anxiety over many months and years before we reach this conclusion, and for more serious problems such as anxiety disorders or severe depression to develop.

Now, in today's society, this learning can take place at a much faster pace. We are surrounded by examples of people who look better, live better and have achieved more than us. We observe more and we compare more. Further experiences of threat and conflict (although they continue to make us feel bad) now become largely irrelevant for we have found the answer.

Anxiety feels bad, we feel bad, and everywhere we turn confirms the reason why – others are better than us; we are not good enough and may be rejected over it.

That explains it; everything fits…

We have anxiety because there is something wrong with us.

But it's not true.

Just like the eagle that thought he was a chicken – it all seems true, but it isn't.

Let's be clear about one thing now. With regard to anxiety and feeling weak, insecure and vulnerable… **we feel this way because of what is happening (or has happened) to us and not because there is something wrong with us.**

PART III

CALM ANXIETY

...

5

Understanding Control
And Change

WHEN IT BECOMES less about the external situation and more about our self, anxiety can be very difficult to deal with. With external threats we have an element of control: we can avoid the situation in the first place, flee from it or fight our way through it. These are classic responses; exactly what anxiety is designed for, to save us from getting hurt. But when much of the anxiety we experience is linked to the way we feel about our self, it can seem as though we have no control at all.

From nervousness and anxiety to panic attacks and phobias; from the obsessive thinking and compulsive behaviours in OCD through to the hopelessness and helplessness of severe depression... the feeling that there is nothing we can do about it plays a massive part in strengthening the problem.

Control

It lies deep within human nature – the need to be in control of our environment. It must, for our very survival depends on it.

We have an innate drive to understand things that influence our lives so that we can have some control over them, some control over our own survival and existence. Any situation that we cannot understand or control remains, in one sense, unresolved and anything could happen. Such situations have the potential to cause us harm and so remain frightening.

This drive has led humans to conquer the oceans, the highest mountains and outer space and we'll search a lifetime to achieve insight into something we feel has power over us. When we have a sense of control over something, we feel safe for we know we can handle whatever may happen. However, the knowledge that we cannot control something, in itself, increases our anxiety over it.

[Nowhere is the effect of feeling 'that we have no control' seen more greatly than in depression. Here, we feel that nothing we do is of any use, we cannot change anything, the world is against us and everything we try fails so what is the point of even trying.

Jewish prisoners in the concentration camps, with no control over any aspect of their lives, came to have no reason to pay attention to anything, even life itself.

In an experiment in the 1970's, dogs were given electric shocks with or without a control lever being available for them to press and stop the shocks. Dogs that had the control lever quickly learned to stop the shocks and also learned new ways (presented to them later) to stop more electric shocks. The dogs that had never had control of the shocks wouldn't learn new ways to stop the shocks when given the opportunity to do so later. They had already learned that they had no control over the situation and simply gave up and accepted all future shocks helplessly – it was a learned helplessness. And it is this, a conditioned helplessness, rather than mental illness, that underpins most people's depression problems today.

Like anxiety, depression is a part of being human that has evolved for our benefit. A slowing down of mind and body systems (emotions and reactions) in times of stress and excitability, over which we have no control, may give us a chance to recuperate rather than continue to burn up resources fruitlessly. The fact that (normal) depression generally fades over time without treatment may support this.

Note that virtually everything that has been said (and will be said) in this book about anxiety also applies to depression. With anxiety problems, life experiences have made us feel scared. With depression problems, life has made us feel scared and helpless. Both are because of what has happened to us and not because something is wrong (or has gone wrong) with us.]

The feeling that we have no control scares us – so much so that we spend our lives trying to be in control; each and every one of us, not just those with anxiety-related problems. Everything is ordered and categorised to help us know what we are dealing with. People are labelled: married or single, employed or unemployed, rich or poor. Superstition, rituals and lucky charms are used to ward off bad luck and gamblers devise systems in attempts to control random outcomes. Lack of control can be so anxiety arousing that our mind will often 'fill in' any gaps in information rather than leave things incomplete and unpredictable. This phenomenon forms the basis of many optical illusions and magic tricks.

Things are no different with anxiety. If avoidance, fighting or fleeing is not an option to resolve our anxiety then, over time, our mind resorts to other ways to regain control. These are often subconscious and can be clearly observed in most long-term anxiety and depression problems. One is 'thinking too much' and the other can best be described as 'how to be'.

Thinking Too Much

Most people with long-term anxiety (and depression) problems would agree that they tend to think too much about things... but why?

Constantly going back over things are attempts to find out why we feel as we do, why we behave as we do and why these things happened to us. They are also attempts to find out what we can do to resolve the situation. They are, in all their forms, essentially efforts to understand and master the problem.

These efforts are usually reflected in other behaviours such as high levels of tidiness, orderliness, list-making and planning – good qualities, which lead to excellent organisational skills, if not taken to extreme.

Also, the ability to look for reasons, draw conclusions and find answers requires a high level of intelligence and this is supported by research that shows that many people with anxiety problems generally exhibit a higher than average level of intelligence.

A Sense of Control by 'How to Be'

When life experiences, conditioning and learning lead us to the conclusion that we are too anxious because there is something wrong with us, and we search constantly for answers to our problem, eventually we do find an answer. We can, we believe, control the fear of being rejected because of 'not being good enough' by being extra 'good' or better in some way. This 'how to be' (which ultimately leads to having to be perfect) can cause us to monitor our actions, feelings, emotions and even our thoughts to try and develop the 'right' way to be.

[Although beyond the scope of this book (check out:- *'Evolving Self Confidence: How to Become Free From Anxiety Disorders and Depression'*) it may be helpful to know that, to a large extent, it is this 'how to be' that defines many anxiety disorders today.

It can be clearly seen in two very common problems. In the eating disorder 'Anorexia Nervosa' personal fears and insecurities are attributed to 'being too fat' resulting in a desperate need to be thin, and in social anxiety disorder feelings of inadequacy lead to an overriding need to be better in some way (bigger, stronger, better looking, brighter etc.).

Of course we all exhibit 'how to be' regularly. We act differently when with our friends, in an interview or on a first date. Here, we use our social learning skills to maximise our chances of being accepted.

The problem arises when 'how to be' becomes much more than this and it turns into a desperate need – a way that we *must* be or act in order to protect our self from attack or rejection.

Over time, maintaining such standards of perfection with which to compare our self to others (and berate our self if we don't meet them) often leads to constant self-monitoring (being overly self-consciousness), increased stress and ultimately that state of extreme anxiousness and fear seen in many anxiety disorders.]

Unfortunately, the things we do to master our anxiety problem (both subconsciously and consciously) actually keeps it alive.

Fighting anxiety, in various ways, merely strengthens it. It's just like those violinists we read about earlier. Reading, researching, experimenting, trying ways to think, trying ways to behave, trying 'how to be' etc., actually increases the number of connections in the brain associated with the problem. Basically, the more we think about our problem and do things connected to it (even in trying to deal with it), the bigger and stronger that part of our brain relating to our problem becomes.

Can we use this knowledge for our benefit?
Is it possible to change?

Change (Weakening the Connections)

Virtually everything we do in our life we have learned. Some reflexes, behaviours, predispositions and aptitudes may result from evolution but even these can be modified and developed through learning. Learning involves a change in the nervous system and gradual automation.

Change in the Nervous System

Experiences shape the patterns of neural connections within our brain and in doing so change us. When we learn something, new connections form within our brain and nervous system. The more things associated with the learning the greater the number and more varied the patterns of neural connections that form. Repetition of the learning leads to the connections occurring more frequently and thus becoming stronger. That is, the stronger the learning, the more it becomes part of our make-up and the way we are.

Take the following simple example: learning the colours of the rainbow.

If we simply learned the seven colours: *Red, Orange, Yellow, Green, Blue, Indigo* and *Violet,* making no associations, the knowledge would not remain in our memory for very long. (Try it and see – write down seven different colours (not the ones in a rainbow) and, without making any associations to aid memory, learn the list until you can repeat it. Put the list somewhere safe and see if you can remember the colours one week later).

However, when we associate the colours of the rainbow with the popular mnemonic: *Richard Of York Gave Battle In Vain* (introducing elements of wonder: who was Richard of York? Which battle did he lose? And a dash of surprise: the cleverness of the connection) our learning becomes that much stronger. In fact the first thing that comes to mind for most people when asked to name the colours in a rainbow is the association itself – 'Richard Of York Gave Battle In Vain'.

It's not really surprising then, that anxiety problems which involve learning associated with a myriad of feelings, thoughts, emotions, confirmations, reasoning, comparisons, evidence and expectations do strongly shape our brain and nervous system, do change our thoughts, feelings and behaviour and do become part of us.

However, this part of us is not an inborn quality nor caused by some mysterious illness. We are not born with low self-confidence and feelings of insecurity; something didn't just go wrong. The same goes for any obsessive thoughts and compulsive behaviours, irrational fears and phobias or feelings of helplessness – these things develop from learning and the conclusions drawn from the evidence in our experiences.

The good news is that the evidence we used was false and the conclusions we drew were wrong. And we can build on what we now know to reshape our nervous system and reshape our life.

Gradual Automation

Behaviours and thought processes that are repeated over and over again gradually become automatic, that is, they can be performed 'without thinking'. Again, related to survival, this has to be the case. Things that we do regularly (have been strongly learned) can be carried out 'automatically' so that our attention is available for anything else that may require it and we are ready to learn new things.

Imagine having to learn from scratch how to drive a car every time you wanted to use it, how to ride a bike, how to swim, how to tie a tie or a shoe lace or having to relearn how to write every time you wanted to compose a letter.

For those who can drive, remember the concentration and practise and even more practise required when you learned to coordinate the clutch, gears and accelerator. Now you do it without even thinking about it – it's automatic.

This process not only applies to behaviours but also to thoughts and memories. Anyone who has ever revised for examinations will have experienced forgetting that section you learned until you remember the first few words, then the rest comes flowing back – automatically.

When behaviours or thought processes are repeated over and over again the associated connections in the brain become so strongly linked that once the behaviour is started the rest follows in sequence as these strongly connected areas of the brain work together. This forms the basis of habits, which are behaviours we do so often that they become automatic. Initially done for a good reason, habitual behaviours often continue through automation and once started, we see them through even though any initial rewards or good feelings associated with the behaviour may no longer apply.

Gradual automation can be seen in many aspects of anxiety problems, in that once the initial feelings occur, all of the associated thoughts, emotions and behaviours generally follow.

Take avoidance for example. Here, the initial mental image of facing the situation can lead to memories of past 'failures' and the expectation of impending 'failure', anticipated feelings of shame and rejection, and the physiological signs of anxiety such as increased heart rate, shaking, dizziness etc.

The thoughts, emotions and behaviours then interact, repeat and strengthen to such a degree that the resultant panic often causes us to avoid the situation in order to obtain relief.

All of this from that first thought; that first spark between neurons in our brain that now connects to all the other neural pathways associated to our problem – neural pathways that we built up through learning.

This understanding of learning shows us how it is possible to change. To change we need to reduce the strength of previously learned thoughts and behaviours and learn new ones. That is, we must weaken the strength of the connections in the brain and nervous system that are associated with insecurity and anxiety and develop and strengthen new connections associated with more positive beliefs – ones that actually reflect the truth.

But how can connections in the nervous system be weakened?

Consider the following:-

Top golfers, snooker and darts players practise their skills relentlessly for many hours every day. This, along with some natural ability, can keep them at the very highest level, perhaps in the top ten, of their sport.

Connections in the brain associated with such things as hand-eye-muscle coordination, body position and balance, and the judgement of distance and speed, need to become strong and stay strong for them to remain at that level. But what happens if they don't practise?

A top class player that does not practise for a month will probably fall out of the top ten rankings and one who does not practise for a year will probably not make the top one hundred. The neural connections in the brain associated with the behaviour have diminished through lack of use and so has the behaviour. That part of the person that was a top class sportsman no longer exists.

This weakening also applies to thought processes. The ability to do simple mathematics can easily be lost through lack of use, as anyone who has forgotten how to do simple multiplication and division problems since the advent of the personal calculator can testify.

Memories, if not recalled, fade with time.

Similarly, limbs can diminish if not used. A broken leg in plaster for six months loses both size and function to some extent and usually needs extensive physiotherapy once the cast is removed.

As the adage goes: *If you don't use it – lose it!*

Connections in the brain and nervous system can be weakened by… **not using them**.

If we don't think those thoughts and don't do those behaviours they will gradually weaken and fade. Of course this is easier said than done. People with anxiety problems can be likened to those top class sportsmen, continually strengthening the connections in their brain by daily practising.

As stated earlier, we have an innate need to solve problems, to have a sense of control, and we do this by continually going over the situation looking for reasons, answers and solutions. In doing so we are continually reinforcing all those connections in our brain associated with the anxiety.

This is one of the main paradoxes with anxiety-related problems (there are more), and one of the reasons that they are so difficult to 'cure' – in continually trying to find an answer to our problem, in continually battling and fighting against our anxiety... we make the problem worse.

However, there is something we can do when our anxiety problem strikes, one thing that stops the whole process in its tracks and prevents all of the associated neural connections coming into play. It goes against every instinct we have when dealing with anxiety but it is the only way to truly control it. The way to control this anxiety is to let go... and we do that by accepting it.

ACCEPTANCE

When we *truly* accept 'anxious' thoughts, feelings and behaviours we can stop strengthening the problem and allow it to fade.

And we are now in a position to truly accept these things because we know exactly what is happening and why. Acceptance without such insight is doomed to failure for the unknown will always overpower us – but we can now accept the truth as we know it. And the truth is: there is nothing wrong with us, we feel this way because of how we were treated in the past; how we mis-interpreted the behaviour of others and how we developed ways to protect our self. We are anxious because of the way we were made to feel and not due to some inherent 'wrongness'.

And from this truth we can now form an acceptance statement (words to the effect of):-

"I know this is happening to me because I have been made to feel scared and led to believe it is because of me. Anyone with my experiences would feel the same. My anxiety is only trying to protect me. I am not bad or wrong in any way, it's only how I was made to feel."

This acceptance statement, based on underlying truth, forms the foundation for change. You need to adapt it and make it personal to you – something that you firmly believe.

Write your statement down and read it for the first few times. (See APPENDIX 1) Include a sentence saying something like, 'anyone would feel the same', for they would, they do – the vast number of people struggling with anxiety problems today confirms this. It's rather ironic that anxiety problems are deemed 'mental illness' when, given many modern-day life experiences, it would be abnormal not to have increased anxiety.

Keep your statement succinct; make it something that 'feels right' for you.

Whenever we start to think, feel or behave in ways associated with our anxiety problem we can stop the process through acceptance. Use it for any 'unexplained' anxiety feeling or symptom or perhaps some negative self-talk. In all of these cases, accepting things stops them, fighting them makes them worse. A trembling hand cannot be stopped by tensing it and trying to force it to stop shaking but it can be stopped by relaxing it. Accepting things is also important for other situations associated with our anxiety. Take, for example, if we catch our self 'thinking too much'. Accepting this would involve saying to our self, something like:-

"I realise that I am trying to find answers for what happened to me, trying to get control but I now know exactly what happened and why."

The same goes for comparing our self to other people excessively or feeling a greater need for 'how to be'. In both of these cases, accepting that our behaviour has good reason prevents things from escalating.

When using your written/main acceptance statement, if possible say it out loud (or under your breath) as this gives it greater form and presence. Doing this can also form the basis of a more understanding and positive self-talk, which will come to be internalised and create an inner reassuring guide rather than a critic.

Acceptance, through something you believe and use regularly can really turn things around. But it must be true acceptance, not just saying the statement and hoping to have no anxiety – this is just trying to avoid it.

We are not saying the statement to make the anxiety go away... we are saying it to accept the anxiety.

...WE HAVE TO HAVE ANXIETY, WE HAVE TO FEEL IT AND WE HAVE TO ACCEPT IT.

Accepting in this way ultimately changes the pattern of connections in our brain. Old patterns weaken and fade and new ones take shape – ones that represent a whole new belief and attitude about our problem. The problem as we know it starts to change, it no longer means the same to us or has the same hold over us.

We are not simply removing our anxiety problem (something that cannot really be done) but changing it. The thoughts and feelings come to us but we let them fade and weaken through acceptance rather than build them up and strengthen them by resisting and fighting.

And this is how we work as humans; confidence and 'holding ones nerve' comes from not dwelling on the negative and not thinking about (hence strengthening) the doubts and fears and feelings. Many confident people when asked about some forthcoming 'big event' (for example, a wedding speech or a work presentation) will reply "I'm trying not to think about it'.

I remember a TV interview with one of the spice girls, Mel C, who, when asked about an imminent awards ceremony, replied: "I try not to think about it otherwise I get too nervous."

In the past our problems revolved around building up and strengthening all those bad thoughts and feelings. Ruminating, worrying, comparing and despairing, and looking for reasons and answers all served to keep the problem alive. These behaviours can be compared to 'picking at a scab' preventing healing. The natural state of the body and mind is one of health and if we don't fight and block it, if we don't keep 'picking away' they will heal.

Through acceptance, we allow our mind (and body) to heal. We accept the thoughts and feelings instead of fighting and resisting them. Of course the effects of acceptance take time, but this too has an analogy with how we work as humans. Building up acceptance can be likened to building up a muscle; the more we take control of our thoughts and feelings, the stronger the ability becomes until it is a part of our nature and self-belief. Over time, a new belief in our strength and ability begins to take shape, and belief is everything.

*

The art of acceptance is even more powerful than this for it underpins two of life's greatest issues. One is facing fears the other is developing self-confidence.

Let's look at facing fearful situations. Here, insight and acceptance form the basis of the psychological technique known as 'systematic desensitisation'.

To overcome fearful situations we need to break down the fear into smaller parts and learn to control it and master it in stages.

Facing Fearful Situations

To overcome fearful situations:-

- Break down your fear into smaller fears.
- Grade these fears on a scale from 1 to 10 (more if you need to). Where 10 = mildly frightening and 1 = extremely frightening.
- Start with number 10. (The weakest fear – so weak that it barely exists.)
- Feel the anxiety, thoughts, feelings etc.
- Accept why they are there and calm yourself down through relaxation and deep breathing (see later).
- Gradually move up the levels of difficulty. But only move to the next level when you have mastered taking control at each level. (Taking control is feeling scared but accepting it, going with it, and calming down not fighting it or running from it).

When using this method we are not doing anything extraordinary. It is no magic technique; what we are doing mirrors life. Everyone masters difficult situations in stages – it is the only way to do it.

Picture a young child approaching the ocean for the first time. First they let the water cover their feet; then, when they feel more confident they move deeper, up to their knees. As confidence develops they move up to their waist and so on...

We are doing nothing more.

*

Acceptance is indeed truly powerful. However, there is something else that we can use to enhance its effect in weakening those neural connections forged in our brain through life experiences. We can distract our self, and this, once again, reflects how we work as humans.

Distraction

The human brain is incredibly complex, comprising around 100 billion brain cells and 100,000 billion connections. But for all this complexity there is an ability we don't possess. That is the ability to pay real attention to more than one thing at a time.

We can do 'automatic' behaviours and attend to something else, (that is the whole point of behaviour becoming automatic) but we cannot give only part of our attention to something that is of importance for this represents a lack of control.

Try the following simple example...

Can you solve the two equations in your head at the same time? Not one then the other or part of one then part of the other but both together simultaneously!

$$84 \div 16 =$$
$$24 \times 17 =$$

If we try to work out (84 ÷16), we cannot think about (24 x 17). If we then shift our attention to (24 x 17), we stop thinking about (84 ÷16). And if we try and do them together, we can't do either. In fact, we cannot do much of anything at all when we are prevented from attending to something fully.

Some may proffer examples such as: people who read on a plane to try and take their mind off phobias about flying, to support the notion that we can attend to two things at once – reading, but still thinking about the fear. In truth, the person's mind has never been taken off the fear, it is the main focus of attention and the reading has never been given true attention. This is shown by what usually happens: they have to read the same sentence or paragraph over and over again because of a lack of attention. The fear indicates a threat, reading doesn't and so real attention is given to the fear. Such people are generally attempting to overcome the fear by distraction alone, which will never work, for this is simply fighting it. Truly accepting the fear (and the reason for it) first then distracting attention by reading would be a better way.

Distraction can be used to supplement acceptance whenever it is sensible, possible or practical to do so. Once we have accepted the reason for the bad thoughts, feelings or behaviours and stopped them from building up and progressing automatically, using distraction can enhance this by moving our thoughts etc. to a different set of neural connections entirely.

Distractions that may be helpful include such things as: reading a book or article, doing a crossword or puzzle, doing something creative (draw or sculpt), speak to a friend on the phone, listen to music, take a bath or go for a walk... anything we can become absorbed in.

* * *

The power of acceptance comes from knowledge and insight, and it grows through understanding. Numerous studies have shown how panic can be tempered through an understanding of what is happening to the body.

Acceptance – using insight into the truth about what is really happening – can help us to change. But don't fight to accept or fight to distract, for this will only strengthen the 'anxiety problem' connections. Just move on and try again next time. Only acceptance that is natural and true (not forced or a 'must do') can work.

To take control we have to let go. Acceptance helps us to do this and confidence grows as the feelings of control grow. However there are even more things that we can do to reduce the anxiety we hold inside – simple steps to take that can have a positive effect deep within us.

...

6

Mind and Body

OUR BODY AND MIND are so intertwined that it's often difficult to distinguish between them; thoughts generate feelings and feelings generate thoughts. Nowhere is this interplay between mind and body demonstrated so convincingly as in the person with anxiety problems. Physical sensations such as tension, shakiness, aches, pains and dullness (whatever their actual cause) can become associated with the thoughts confirming worthlessness, which leads to an increase in those sensations, which further increases the confirming thoughts, which further increases the sensations... and so on. The vicious circle is set up. It's not surprising that we can spend most of the day thinking and feeling bad!

If we are good to our mind, our body feels good and if we are bad to our mind our body feels bad. Similarly, treating our body badly hurts our mind just as treating it well can promote a sense of well-being.

We know that we feel worse when we are tense, unfit, eating poorly and not sleeping well and these factors can all play a part in any symptoms that we experience. Hence there are things we can do that will influence our nervous system in a deep, positive way. These include: Relaxation, Exercise, Diet and Sleep (**REDS**).

RELAXATION

Anxiety leads to tension but also tension leads to anxiety. Most people with long-term anxiety exist in a higher than average state of tension, and a tense body is already making the association with self-protection, 'prepared' to spark off a worrying thought or image and start the ball rolling towards panic, phobias, obsessions, compulsions or despair.

[The upper chest and shoulders is one area where many people with anxiety-related problems maintain tension in their body. They constantly have raised upper chest and shoulders. This is for two reasons: firstly, it is a defensive posture (I would raise my shoulders if somebody went to strike me) and secondly, it stems from a conditioning associated with the body's attempt to relieve tension naturally through sighing. Letting out a deep breath is a natural way to relieve tension.

Many people with these problems hold their breath a lot (especially before going to sleep) in order to sigh.

This can lead to conditioning the body to have the chest and shoulders constantly raised and also to the development of breathing from the chest rather than the diaphragm.

Try this:- throughout the day notice how high your shoulders are and drop them down (or, as in Yoga - 'roll them over and back').

When your shoulders are lowered – do you feel ever so slightly more relaxed? Do this a number of times throughout the day and when you are in bed before you go to sleep.]

Relaxation is the opposite of tension.
A muscle that is relaxed cannot be tense.
We can reduce tension by learning to relax.

This is something that we must do. We have to reduce the tension inside us, for when we exist in a state of 'background' tension our anxiety problem is essentially with us all the time.

We may feel that being unable to relax *is* the problem, but it's not that we cannot relax, it is just that it is very, very difficult given that we have learned so strongly to be tense and prepared.

Learning to relax involves learning how various parts of the body feel when they are tense and relaxing them.

Numerous methods exist and one of the most widely used is the Progressive Muscle Relaxation Technique. First described in the 1920's by Edmund Jacobsen, this involves systematically tensing and relaxing various groups of muscles. (See APPENDIX 2)

You need to find a method that you feel comfortable with and then practise, practise and practise some more until relaxing becomes a strongly learned behaviour and being calm and relaxed becomes the natural state rather than being tense.

Relaxing the body relaxes the mind and relaxing the mind relaxes the body. This is shown at times when we are engrossed in some activity such as reading, writing, painting or watching a movie and our mind is taken off the problem completely. When we're not thinking about our problem we are more relaxed both mentally and physically.

The aim is to become more relaxed in general but there is also something we can do that can help us to relax 'in the moment'. It is something mentioned with regard to facing fearful situations and can be used in conjunction with acceptance. It is: deep-breathing.

Deep Diaphragmatic Breathing

As we learned earlier, one of the main symptoms associated with anxiety (and panic) is breathing too fast.

The effort to get oxygen-rich blood to our major muscles quickly can lead to hyperventilation, in which the oxygen-carbon dioxide balance in our bloodstream becomes disrupted. Exhaling carbon dioxide too fast can make us feel as though we can't breathe and actually increase any anxiety or panic that we experience.

The way to counteract this is to breathe slowly and deeply from the diaphragm rather than the chest.

By replacing the fast, upper-chest breathing of anxiety and panic with deep slow breathing, where we breathe from the diaphragm (the muscular wall separating the lungs from the stomach) we redress the O_2-CO_2 balance in the body and promote a feeling of calmness.

Try deep diaphragmatic breathing:-

1.   Take a slow deep breath in through your nose for a slow count of four (imagine the air filling your stomach, not lungs, and feel it expand).
2.   Hold for a slow count of four.
3.   Breathe out through your mouth for a slow count of four (imagine your stomach pushing the air out).
4.   Hold for a slow count of four.
5.   Repeat 3 or 4 times, no more.

How do you feel? With practice you can use this technique to calm down in those times you feel anxious or panicky where there is no real danger.

Diaphragmatic breathing is known as eupnea. It is a natural and relaxed form of breathing found in all mammals whenever they are in a state of relaxation and free from danger in their environment.

A very important thing to realise about this is the key role of insight. Knowing what is happening (and why) dramatically increases the power of the technique – just telling someone who is panicking to breathe more slowly and deeply doesn't have the same effect. The same goes for exercise.

EXERCISE

Exercise helps to keep our bodies in good condition. As well as toning and strengthening the muscles it helps improve circulation and lower blood pressure. It can, however, place a great deal of stress and strain on the body and in order to counteract this the body produces its own stress-relieving chemicals known as endorphins. These morphine-related painkillers, produced to relieve the stresses and strains of exercise, act on the nervous system in general and help to promote feelings of relaxation and well-being.

Numerous studies have shown the benefits of regular exercise for dealing with anxiety and depression problems. In many cases exercise helped just as much as, if not more than, medication. Here's how it can help...

Exercise and Anxiety

Anxiety often leads to worrying. This represents a form of inaction: something is making us anxious and we are not doing anything about it, just worrying. In exercising we promote the feeling of actually doing something and also provide an outlet for the build up of nervous energy.

Physically: we are using up all of the nervous energy (adrenaline etc.) produced by anxiety in order to prepare us for action (to fight or run away) – nervous energy that could turn into worry if not used.

Mentally: we are actually doing something, taking action (even though it's not connected to our problem) rather than just sitting about worrying.

Regarding anxiety, exercise can reduce the fears over physical sensations such as a racing heart and rapid breathing. This can be extremely beneficial in the gym situation where the social aspect can lead to an acceptance of these body sensations (and fears about them) in the presence of other people.

Exercise and Depression

With depression we can come to feel that everything we do is hopeless and doomed to fail, so much so that we no longer even try. Because of this, our body stops producing energy and we get into a cycle of not doing things and having no energy to do anything.

The more we do, the more energy our body produces to enable us to do it. (Exercising for one hour, though tiring, fills us with energy whilst lazing about makes us feel lethargic with no energy to do anything.) When we exercise we are doing something.

Physically: we are taking action, doing something, and our body will now start to provide us with more energy naturally.

Mentally: we are actually doing something, anything (even though it is not connected to our problem) rather than just sitting about 'obsessing'.

Studies have shown that, in some cases, exercise can be more beneficial for depression than medication. And this makes sense for it counteracts the 'having no energy' and 'doing nothing' parts of depression like no drug can.

*

Exercise not only builds physical strength but mental strength too. It increases resilience to the stresses of daily living and the feelings of achievement it promotes can empower us. Other benefits include:-

- Increased fitness
- Weight control
- Improves appearance and self-image
- Increased social contact
- Helps to relax us
- Improved posture
- Promotes a positive mental attitude
- Improved function of all vital organs (including the brain)

Exercising regularly really is one of the best things we can do to improve many areas in our life, however:

ALWAYS CONSULT A MEDICAL PROFESSIONAL BEFORE STARTING ANY EXERCISE REGIME.

Generally speaking:-

- Do something that you enjoy. Exercise should be enjoyable (and challenging). Setting goals, short workouts, listening to music and doing it with friends – these things can make it more fun.
- Start slowly, don't overdo it.
- Do it regularly: 3 to 4 times a week (10–60 mins).
- Don't focus on the aches and pains during exercise. Think how good you will feel when you have finished.

And:

ALWAYS SEEK QUALIFIED ADVICE TO ENSURE THAT YOU EXERCISE AT THE APPROPRIATE LEVEL FOR YOUR AGE AND FITNESS.
(eg. from a gym instructor).

As we get fitter our resting heartbeat rate becomes slower, something that, in itself, makes us calmer.

Even gentle exercise such as walking (briskly and often) can provide many of the same benefits. Or consider Yoga, which combines both relaxation and exercise.

Relaxation and exercise are two ways in which we can take real action to decrease the amount of stress and strain in our body and mind. The next thing we will look at can easily increase those stresses and strains, even though we may not realise it. It's what we eat.

DIET

There's a small grey tree frog that lives in the Baskett Wildlife Area, near Ashland, Missouri. In the late 1990's the population of tree frogs began to die out. Locals blamed a then new pesticide that had recently been introduced into the area, but the makers of the chemical conducted tests in the laboratory, exposing the frogs to the pesticide, and showed that it did not affect them.

However, later experiments conducted by the University of Pittsburgh showed something extremely interesting: the pesticide did indeed appear harmless to the tree frogs in the tranquil setting of the laboratory but when the frogs were exposed to the pesticide *and* the stress of daily living in their natural environment (particularly those stresses related to predators) the combination proved lethal. The compound effect of stress in the environment and pesticide chemicals proved just too much for the frog's immune system.

And the same applies to us, humans.

Man-made chemicals, many of which are extremely toxic (pesticides), used throughout the food production process undoubtedly create added stresses and strains (probably at a cellular level) on our body and mind.

Only in the last one hundred years or so has our nervous system had to deal with this onslaught and it may explain the drastic increase of once uncommon physical illnesses that we see in society today.

One thing is for sure: when we are struggling with conflict and stress due to anxiety (and depression) and the resultant damage they cause, the last thing we need is any additional strain on our system.

In order to minimise the stress that we suffer we need to reduce the burden of man-made chemicals in our body. Remember, these are compounds that the human body has never had to deal with before.

Good dietary advice for everyone (not just those with anxiety-related problems) really is clear-cut: reduce or eliminate refined and processed food from your diet. The more something is processed, the more we should avoid it. Eat fresh, natural, wholesome foods whenever possible (organically produced?). A good, well-balanced, varied diet that includes nothing more than the six essential nutrients of water, carbohydrates, proteins, fats, vitamins, and minerals can help us tremendously. As with relaxation and exercise, a good diet promotes both physical and mental health.

Remember:

ALWAYS CONSULT A MEDICAL PROFESSIONAL BEFORE STARTING ANY NEW DIET REGIME.

Relaxation, exercise and a good diet... practising these regularly will reap great rewards. But there's one more thing that we need to consider. We spend around one third of our life doing it and it's very, very important to our overall well-being... sleeping.

SLEEP

Although the exact function of sleep is still under question, one thing we can be fairly sure of is that it performs a restorative function. We know from personal experience that people who go for long periods without sufficient sleep can be irritable, on edge, unable to concentrate and feel confused.

Lack of sleep may affect our emotional ability to withstand stress and most people believe that they 'feel better' after a good night's sleep. It appears that most of us require 8 or 9 hours of sleep to be free from daytime sleepiness.

When we have difficulty in falling asleep, it may be a good idea to accept what is happening rather than fight to get to sleep. Whether it's due to 'thinking too much', planning or worrying or because our mind is trying to sort out lots of information from the day... whatever the reason for it, acceptance, once again, can prevent things from getting worse.

There are many tips available regarding getting a good night's sleep. Find and practise the ones that are comfortable and helpful to you. Here's a few ideas:-

Don't (just before bedtime):-

- Take alcohol or caffeine – these can disrupt the sleep cycle and cause you to wake early.
- Eat heavily – this causes the digestive system to be active during the night.
- Do heavy exercise or brainwork or rush around.

Do:-

- Slow down around one hour before bed.
- Try and relax – engage in soothing activities (eg. a warm bath, light reading, soft music).
- Establish a regular routine – go to bed around the same time each night and wake up around the same time each morning.
- Ensure the bedroom is not too light or dark and is a comfortable temperature.

*

In learning and maintaining good habits regarding relaxation, exercise, diet and sleep we can take real, practical steps to positively influence our body, mind and nervous system. You need to explore ways that are comfortable and beneficial to you and do them regularly until they become good, strong, habitual behaviours.

Incidentally, people who feel good about themselves do these things as a matter of course, out of self-respect.

Take care not to treat these things as 'how to be'; we are not doing them to be 'right' in any way. Remember you don't have to do anything to be right for you are okay just as you are. We do these things to reduce and change what has happened to our body and mind in the past. They are simple, practical steps that, when coupled with insight and acceptance, can have a profound, long-lasting effect on how we feel.

As the old connections associated with our problem start to fade and new ones take shape, there is one more very important thing that we need to address. That is: the situation (or situations) responsible for our problem in the first place.

Continuous conflict within the family, school, work or social environment feeds our insecurity and makes everything much more difficult, therefore we need to remove this conflict from our life.

To do this, we have three options: *avoid it, stop it* or *change it*.

In theory, we could stop being bullied by having the bully removed from school or the workplace, or avoid it by changing schools or jobs. Perhaps we could get the bully to change by talking to them.

In reality, life isn't that easy. There are many common situations that we simply cannot stop, avoid or change. Indeed, it's the fact that we are trapped (with no control) that contributes enormously to the problem.

However, there is one thing we can do that changes any situation (even ones from the past that still hurt us) – we can change what we think about it and how we let it affect us. For it's not what happens to us that damages the most, it is what we make of it.

With this in mind, let's consider some common conflict situations and what is really going on.

• Re: Parental Criticism

Our parents are big, we are small; they are strong and we are weak; they know things we don't, therefore we really must be 'stupid', 'useless' etc.

Some parents can't help themselves. They cannot stop themselves being angry and critical of a child whose imperfections they believe reflect on them. They are driven by their own feelings of weakness and self-doubt.

Are such parents really weak? Are they not strong and it's the child that is weak? Well, consider this…

Without exception, those who criticise others can rarely take criticism themselves and they never fail to tell us just how good they are as they berate us. Most of them would never (dare) say to another adult, the things they say to us and are often kinder to strangers than they are to their own family.

If we were actually behaving in a way that was bad or wrong, a strong parent would explain why it was wrong and show us the correct behaviour; they would guide and support us in order to help us improve. They certainly wouldn't make us feel humiliated and ashamed. Many of our parents have greater problems than we realise. They are angry and frustrated at their own lives and they hate it, they don't hate us – it just feels as though they do.

Regarding parental criticism, there are two important things to realise. Firstly: parents are often doing the best they can given their own problems, and secondly: whenever they (or anyone else for that matter) call you 'stupid', 'useless' etc. in a harsh, angry way – they are actually saying it about themselves.

• Re: Bullying

Strong people don't pick on others, belittle other people or hurt them. Why should they? They are strong and secure within themselves and don't need to hurt others because of their own inner pain.

With bullying, it is very important not to add to any actual physical pain with self-created (and usually far worse) emotional pain, and realise that it is the bully who is truly weak and not us. It shows not strength but weakness to attack somebody who cannot fight back. Bullies are indeed weak and inadequate where it counts most – in mind and in spirit.

• Re: Religion

It's hard to imagine the number of people that live their lives ruled by fear over punishment by God.

But how do we come by such a fear of the Almighty? Does it come from God himself? No, it's always from another human being. How dare any human presume to speak for God and tell us what God will do to us?

Remember this whenever someone is telling you how God is going to punish you.

• Re: Comparing With Others

As we have learned, it is natural to compare our self with others and even to limit our comparisons to those people we consider to be 'better' than us, when we feel inadequate is some way.

But the comparisons we make are totally false for our judgements are based on 'snapshots' of other people. We compare our whole life to a mere fraction of the other person's existence.

How can such judgements be reliable? The happy joker in school may have a life of misery at home; the kind, loving father in public may beat his kids in private. Images are touched up – we never see models with spots or bad hair – and the 'stars' on Facebook etc. are simply acting to be 'liked' and followed.

Whenever you feel the need to compare your self with people that you believe are 'better', remember: what you are comparing your self to is false. Indeed, the only person you ever need to compare your self to is *you*. Strive to be/do better than the previous day and soon all other comparisons will become insignificant.

[When we feel bad about our self and make comparisons with others, we often believe that they are happier than us. The worse we feel, the more we think we have to change in order to achieve this happiness and feel better.

People change jobs, homes and partners looking to feel better and be happy. Yet study after study shows that happiness doesn't come from such radical changes. It's the little things that count, such as appreciating things and expressing gratitude. There are many things that we can do to make us feel a bit happier and better about our self. (See APPENDIX 7)]

- **Re: Peers, Groups and Friends**

Adopting the correct attitude in relation to stressful situations applies in many areas of life. When dealing with other people, remember: it's those who would hurt you that have the problem and no person can truly make accurate comparisons with another.

However, there is one important area of our life that we can actually change – that is the company we keep.

Stay away from toxic people, they'll suck the strength right out of you. Surround your self with people who challenge, encourage and support you.

With friends, it's quality not quantity that counts. One true friend is better than a thousand false ones. (See APPENDIX 6)

*

The above tips are ideas and guidelines, not rigid rules about how to think and behave. Hopefully it is becoming clear that whenever someone hurts you, it is he or she who has the problem, not you.

(It can be comforting to know that when someone is angry with us for no good reason, it's usually themselves they are angry with.)

It is an age-old truth, played out generation after generation in theatres and cinemas across the world, one covered by the music and literature of many different cultures – the weakest people hurt us the most. But never again should the weakness of others hurt you, for now you can deal with such people from a position of wisdom and strength. In conflict situations, you may feel insecure and afraid, justifiably so, but it's not because of any problem with you.

*

There is no doubt about it (whatever we attribute it to) that: when we think positively, we attract positive things into our life, and when we think negatively, life becomes dominated by negative events. And so there is one more thing to consider... negative thoughts.

• Re: Negative Thoughts

"I can't do it." "I'm useless." "Everything I do fails." People tell us to 'just stop thinking like that'. Of course, if we could, we would, but it's not as simple as this for they are more than just thoughts, they are feelings and beliefs.

However, there is one thing we can do that helps to make such thoughts less negative and it involves the use of one small word... 'but'.

Adding 'but' and a qualifying statement to negative thoughts reduces their power slightly by making them less definite, less crushingly final.

"I can't do it... but that might change." "I'm useless... but maybe that's not true." – Whenever you catch your self thinking awful, negative thoughts try adding a qualifier, just a general one that doesn't even involve you and merely considers that things as you see them at the moment may change or may not be true.

Over time, as the connections in the brain associated with anxiety (or depression) problems begin to weaken and fade, negative thoughts will fade naturally for they are simply no longer relevant.

* * *

"The question is not how to get cured, but how to live."
...Joseph Conrad

Life can make us scared. Events, circumstance and the environment all conspire to leave us feeling insecure and vulnerable for much of the time. And we had little choice in the matter, for it is simply what happened to us. Now, through insight and understanding, there is a choice – we can take back control and create a life less anxious.

Accepting (and distracting), relaxing often, exercising regularly, eating good food, sleeping well, refusing to make comparisons (especially via TV or social media) and not letting the weakness of others hurt you should become a new way of life. And the result will be a new, stronger, more positive, self-assured you.

We are all different and yet, in one sense, we are all the same. We all have similar body structures; we all have similar mind structures; we all have the same five senses and we receive and process information through these senses and structures in a very similar manner. Therefore, it is not surprising that we all tend to deal with certain situations in roughly the same way.

Basic truths apply to all, however our individuality and uniqueness means that: 'one size doesn't fit all' so take the advice given and tweak it, mould and shape it to suit your self.

Don't try and force things for only things that you are comfortable with will work. And build up slowly – it's not possible to go from being extremely anxious to being self-assured overnight, just like it isn't possible to run a marathon after twenty years without exercise.

Indeed this analogy shows us just how it is possible to change. For example, it may seem impossible to many people to jog 5 miles, but if we build up slowly by: walking half a mile regularly, then a mile; then jogging 200 yards, then half a mile, then a mile etc. – over time jogging 5 miles becomes easy. The task has not changed, but we have.

The key to success is practise. Practise, practise and practise some more. Most things in life are difficult when we first start but they become easier with effort and practise. However, we need to look at two obstacles that we all face in life and how best to approach them.

Setbacks and Failure

Setbacks are inevitable whenever we try to weaken strongly learned behaviours, just as they are inevitable in all walks of life. We are often quick to attribute setbacks to personal weakness (and any success down to luck), which couldn't be further from the truth, and we do this because of how we feel about failure.

The fear of failure is really the fear of punishment. To a 'normal' person failure may mean 'embarrassment', 'feeling a bit silly' and 'giving a poor performance', but to those of us struggling with anxiety, it can be a crushing blow. It means 'public disclosure of weakness' and lack of ability, which only increases the bad feelings associated with rejection and punishment.

But there is no such thing as failure. Efforts that don't succeed are learning experiences. Learn from them and improve. The only real failure is not to try.

It is only what we associate with failing that makes it so strong. Accept why you feel so bad about it and let it go.

Setbacks can actually help us to learn 'acceptance' more quickly. Accept them for what they are – attempts that didn't quite work out – and move on. They don't reflect your quality as a person. Whenever setbacks arise, practise accepting them. Remember that changing any strongly learned behaviour is difficult (any habit is hard to break) and never associate disappointing results with some 'inherent badness or weakness'.

Know that any success is due to your efforts; things did not happen by chance, you made them happen. Eventually the successes will outnumber the failures and when this happens your confidence will soar.

* * *

It would be nice if, when were scared, someone close came up to us, gave us a cuddle a made us feel safe by assuring us that it's not our fault, there's nothing wrong with us and it's all because of the situation in which we find our self.

Anxiety (and depression) problems are, on the whole, due to what has happened to us and not because of something going wrong in our brain.

Believe this, and change will follow. And here are two more things that you should really believe for they are true:-

People come in various shapes and sizes and have different abilities, talents, strengths and weaknesses but each and every one of us is special...

"You are the amazing product of centuries of evolution and experience, one in six billion that can never be repeated. No other person on the entire planet can think, experience and feel the way you do. You are yourself; that is all there is. That is all there needs to be, just you... for you are unique."

And regarding comparing your self to others…

In this world of manipulated imagery, with examples of 'attractive and successful' people all around us, I'd like to leave you with one final thought. It's a lovely quote (from an unknown source) and in my opinion best expresses one basic truth that we should all adhere to:-

"Search for a beautiful heart, not necessarily a beautiful face. Beautiful people are not always good but good people are always beautiful."

...

...

ACCEPTANCE STATEMENT

_____

_____

_____

_____

_____

_____

_____

_____

_____

_____

- Compose your own acceptance statement.
- Make it personal to you, something that you believe and are comfortable with.
- Include a bit about 'anyone would feel the same', for they would.
- Read the statement out loud the first few times you use it.
- Remember, just try and accept the feelings. We are looking for true acceptance and not a 'forced' or 'hoped for' acceptance.

The Progressive Muscle Relaxation Technique
(Edmund Jacobsen)

This technique can help to create a state of relaxation in both body and mind. It involves tensing certain parts of the body then immediately relaxing them, which promotes greater awareness of (and control over) these two states.

Many variations of the basic concept exist – here's one from the author Joy Rains that can be found on the 'healthline' website:-

Feet

1. Bring your attention to your feet.
2. Point you feet downward and curl your toes under.
3. Tighten your toe muscles gently, but don't strain.
4. Notice the tension for a few moments, then release and notice the relaxation. Repeat.
5. Become aware of the difference between the muscles when they're tensed and when they're relaxed.
6. Continue to tense and relax the leg muscles from the foot to the abdomen area.

Abdomen

1. Gently tighten the muscles of your abdomen, but don't strain.
2. Notice the tension for a few moments. Then release, and notice the relaxation. Repeat.
3. Become aware of the difference between the tensed muscles and the relaxed muscles.

Shoulders and neck

1. Very gently shrug your shoulders straight up towards your ears. Don't strain.
2. Feel the tension for a few moments, release, and then feel the relaxation. Repeat.
3. Notice the difference between the tensed muscles and the relaxed muscles.
4. Focus on the neck muscles, first tensing and then relaxing until you feel total relaxation in this area.

- Find somewhere quiet and comfortable.
- Start with some deep breathing first, to help relax you a little.
- Session should take 20-30 mins.

Diaphragmatic Breathing

The Method:-

1. Take a slow deep breath in through your nose for a slow count of four (imagine the air filling your stomach, not lungs, and feel it expand).
2. Hold for a slow count of four.
3. Breathe out through your mouth for a slow count of four (imagine your stomach pushing the air out).
4. Hold for a slow count of four.
5. Repeat 3 or 4 times, no more.

Facing Fearful Situations

_____

_____

_____

_____

_____

_____

_____

_____

_____

_____

_____

_____

_____

- Break the fear into 10 (or more) parts.
- Grade these fears from strongest to weakest **1** to **10** (or more if necessary).
- Start at the weakest. Only move up the fears when you have experienced the fear, control it (using acceptance and relaxation) and feel the confidence in controlling it.

UNIQUE YOU

You are the amazing product of centuries of evolution and experience, one in six billion that can never be repeated. No other person on the entire planet can think, experience and feel the way you do. You are yourself; that is all there is. That is all there needs to be, just you... for you are unique.

What Makes a True Friend?

- Underline 8 of the qualities below that you feel best represents a **true** friend:-

Intelligent	Considerate	Attractive	Sincere
Sensitive	Rich	Supportive	Discreet
Determined	Honest	Friendly	Domineering
Powerful	Forceful	Trusting	Meticulous
Loyal	Successful	Principled	Understanding

- Circle those qualities that someone who knows you well would say you possess.

Things That Make Us Feel Good

Here's a list (you can probably think of more):-

> **Achieve something.** (Set realistic achievable goals)

> **Create something.** (Baking, crafts, hobbies etc.)

> **Look at, listen to, taste, touch, smell something you like.**

> **Read or watch something inspiring or funny.**

> **List and think about your past achievements.**

> **Check out those personal qualities of a good person that you highlighted previously and feel good about them.**

> **Spend more time with people who make you feel good.**

  (And less time with those who make you feel bad)

> **Be kind to somebody.**

> **Genuinely praise someone who deserves it.**

> **Think about people who like you and how they have shown it.**

> **Spend more time with people who like you.**

  (And less time with those who don't)

> **Sing at the top of your voice (along to music).** (In private)

> **Dance with abandonment.** (In private)

> **Practise REDS** (relaxation, exercise, diet, sleep) **continuously.**

> **Smile more.**

> **Play with a pet.**

> **Help somebody / help out in the community.**

> **Wear something you really like.**

Cont...

> Call up a friend.

> Give something to charity.

> Appreciate beauty.

> Appreciate strength and bravery.

> Apologise for anything that you need to.

> Relive your best ever memory.

> Remember anytime somebody complimented you or showed that they liked you.

> Treat others how you would want them to treat you.

> Meditate.

> Get back to nature. (Go for walks / plant things)

> Do something you are good at – OFTEN.

> Learn a new skill.

> Do something that you have been putting off for a while.

> Clean / tidy / organise something. (Not obsessively)

> Practise gratitude. Be grateful for what you have.

• When you feel good, notice it and accept it.

MORE HELP

If you have had increased anxiety for a long time and are now beginning to experience:-

- Intrusive worrying thoughts that are getting more difficult to stop.
- Obsessive thoughts that are becoming uncontrollable.
- The need to do certain behaviours regularly or starting rituals.
- Irrational fears and phobias (particularly over being seriously ill or doing things in front of others).
- Feelings of helplessness or hopelessness that nothing you do can make a difference.

Or you have suffered for years with full blown:-

GAD
OCD
Panic Disorder
Social Phobia
Severe Depression

You may like to check out:
Evolving Self Confidence: How to Become Free From Anxiety Disorders and Depression

ISBN: 978-0-9558136-0-3
Publisher: Help-For
Author: Terry Dixon
Pages: 288

'Evolving Self Confidence...' presents a totally new way to understand and deal with anxiety disorders and severe depression, showing how to cure the very cause of these problems not just the symptoms.

It takes us on a journey from childhood to adult, through the experiences, thoughts and feelings that can lead to the development of these problems – how they evolve and grow, which disorders develop and why, how we strengthen them and how they become part of us.

And then, the answer... how to turn them around, to evolve and grow through them, beyond them to become stronger and wiser for our experiences... beyond them to become the unique, worthy individual that it is our birthright to be.

AFTERWORD

Today's society and the situations that we encounter in life can provide us with ample opportunity to become anxious and depressed. Nothing else is required.

However, there is one thing, not covered in this book, which can (and does) greatly influence this situation, that is: recreational drugs.

There are many available (including alcohol) but one in particular, cannabis, has become the drug of choice for many people to help them 'chill' and relax.

With its ease of use, low cost and ready supply, younger and younger people use it regularly, and cries go out for its use to be legalised for it is harmless. It isn't.

With all drugs that artificially alter the state of the mind there is one inescapable fact: use them often enough and soon the normal state of mind is no longer normal. If someone uses drugs regularly to relax, when they are not on the drug (not artificially relaxed) the normal world becomes a much scarier place. This is something shown in the paranoia that is frequently exhibited by regular drug users.

Anxiety (and depression) problems and the frequent use of recreational drugs don't mix. Whilst such drugs may seem to offer relief from these problems initially, soon they make things a whole lot worse.

*

Research shows that over 50% of anxiety disorders start before the age of fourteen. (I reckon it's more like 90%).

But some may point to clear examples where anxiety disorders have started later in life. It seems to happen in some cases of GAD and OCD, but we'll consider a more precise example, PTSD.

What of the soldier in his 20's, 30's or 40's that develops PTSD as a direct result of some horrific war experience?

Well, not every soldier who experiences the horrors of war develops PTSD so there must be something else at play. It probably depends on where the person starts out, emotionally. Those that have experienced feelings of insecurity and vulnerability earlier in life must be more susceptible to developing post traumatic stress disorder later in life (under certain conditions). The same goes for generalized anxiety and obsessive-compulsive disorders.

The way we feel about our self in adolescence can stay with us a lifetime. To that end, I believe that all 12/13 year olds should be taught about anxiety and emotions and feelings and why the feel as they do (and what to do about it), in school. I feel that this is a vital part of education given the world we live in today and could 'nip in the bud' any potential anxiety (and depression) related mental health issues for many teenagers.

Future generations don't have to suffer with anxiety and depression problems.

*

Regarding anxiety and depression and mental illness. I would like to point out that what is said in this book is in no way meant to diminish the severity of these problems. Chronic anxiety and depression problems are truly terrible, they cost millions and millions of people the best part of their lives; they cost some their life.

But they are not mental illnesses; mental health issues, yes – it's not right to live life in fear – but something doesn't just go wrong in our brain causing abnormal behaviours.

Labelling anxiety and depression issues (that can be fully explained by conditioning and learning) as mental illness is rapidly creating a society that is dependent on medication, where emotional and life issues have now become illnesses that merit treatment, usually in the form of a pill. This consigns millions of people to a life of helplessness and hopelessness, never actually 'curing' the problem but simply chasing any elusive bit of relief they can find.

End stigma – an honourable cause, sadly misguided.

"Please treat me (with my mental illness) as you would if I had a physical illness." Clinging to this belief, society is rushing further and further down a path that is heading in totally the opposite direction to the real solution for these problems.

To truly end stigma (and literally ease the suffering of millions of people at a stroke) we should stop calling these problems mental illnesses now, and call them something else, something that actually reflects the truth of a normal, healthy person with a normal, healthy mind, being conditioned into a life of anxiety and fear due to personal experience.

My suggestion would be something like: COSI – (a) Conditioned Overactive Survival Instinct.

"I don't have a mental illness, I have a COSI because of my life experiences. I know why it happened and how it happened and I can move beyond it to become a much stronger person for those experiences."

Personal Note from the Author

I have spent over thirty years researching anxiety-related problems – how and why they develop and how to resolve them. A lifetime's search, this involved gaining qualifications in psychology, taking courses on different treatment methods and reading hundreds, if not thousands, of books and websites (both academic and personal stories). During this search, one day it suddenly struck me that: deep down, everyone was saying the same thing.

I would like to thank all of those people who have ever contributed to the collective wisdom of these problems through reading, researching, teaching, writing, treating, experiencing and suffering. Without our combined knowledge this book could not have been written. Thank you.

Terry Dixon